FOOTBALL

FOOTBALL

Subhash K. Goyal

CRESCENT
PUBLISHING CORPORATION

[*The responsibility for the facts stated, conclusions reached and plagiarism, if any, in this book is entirely that of the Author. And the Publisher bears no responsibility for them, whatsoever.*]

Football

First Published : 2009

ISBN 978-81-8342-152-2

Published by :

CRESCENT PUBLISHING CORPORATION
4831/24, Prahlad Street,
Ansari Road, Darya Ganj,
New Delhi - 110002
Ph. : 23272541, 23257835
Fax : 91-011-23257835
e-mail : campusbooks@hotmail.com

Printed at :
Roshan Offset Printers
Delhi

Preface

A ball game which is unique due to its restriction on the use of hands, football is probably the most popular sport in the world today. Two teams of 11 players attempt to guide an inflated ball into goal cages at opposite ends of a playing field, while the other ten players must advance the ball using primarily their feet, although a proficient soccer player can use almost every part of the body, including the head, to control the ball. The continuous action and fast pace of football have made it a major spectator sport throughout the world, and for the same reasons it has attracted millions of players, which includes such legends as Pele and Maradona.

This book concentrates it focus on the most undisputedly popular sport of the world, football. Embarking on a lively, comprehensive and vivid description of the sport's history, the book charts the development and progress of the field since its inception, and details its major tournaments, especially the World Cup, the important players of this sporting arena, and the moments that changed and shaped football forever. In addition, it also engages in an incisive and critical discussion and understanding of contemporary football, dealing with its issues and problems in an enlightening manner. We hope that the book's erudition and insight is well received by football enthusiasts.

Subhash K. Goyal

Contents

1

Introduction to Football

Association football, commonly known as football or soccer, is a team sport played between two teams of 11 players each. It is widely considered to be the most popular sport in the world. Football is a ball game played on a rectangular grass or artificial turf field, with a goal at each of the short ends. The object of the game is to score by manoeuvring the ball into the opposing goal. In general play, the goalkeeper is the only player allowed to use their hands or arms to propel the ball; the rest of the team usually use their feet to kick the ball into position, while they may also occasionally use their torso or head to intercept a ball in mid air. The team that scores the most goals by the end of the match wins. If the score is tied at the end of the game, either a draw is declared or the game goes into extra time and/or a penalty shootout, depending on the format of the competition.

The modern game was codified in England following the formation of the Football Association, whose 1863 Laws of the Game created the foundations for the way the sport is played today. Football is governed internationally by the Fédération Internationale de Football Association (International Federation of Association Football), which is commonly known by the acronym FIFA. The most prestigious international football competition is the World Cup, held every four years. This event, the most widely viewed and famous in the world, boasts an audience twice that of the Summer Olympics.

Nature of the Game

Football is played in accordance with a set of rules, known as the Laws of the Game. The game is played using a single round ball (the *football*) and two teams of eleven players each compete to get the ball into the other team's goal, thereby scoring a goal. The team that has scored more goals at the end of the game is the winner; if both teams have scored an equal number of goals, then the game is a draw.

The primary rule is that the players (other than the goalkeepers) may not deliberately handle the ball with their hands or arms during play (though they do use their hands during a throw-in restart). Although players usually use their feet to move the ball around, they may use any part of their bodies other than their hands or arms.

In typical game play, players attempt to propel the ball toward their opponents' goal through individual control of the ball, such as by dribbling, passing the ball to a team-mate, and by taking shots at the goal, which is guarded by the opposing goalkeeper. Opposing players may try to regain control of the ball by intercepting a pass or through tackling the opponent who controls the ball; however, physical contact between opponents is limited. Football is generally a free-flowing game, with play stopping only when the ball has left the field of play, or when play is stopped by the referee. After a stoppage, play recommences with a specified restart.

At a professional level, most matches produce only a few goals. For example, during the English 2005–06 season of the FA Premier League, an average of 2.48 goals per match were scored.

The Laws of the Game do not specify any player positions other than goalkeeper, but a number of player specialisations have evolved. Broadly, these include three main categories: strikers, or forwards, whose main task is to score goals; defenders, who specialise in preventing their opponents from scoring; and midfielders, who dispossess the opposition and keep possession of the ball in order to pass it to the forwards; players in these positions are referred to as outfield players, in order to discern them from the single goalkeeper. These positions are further differentiated by which side of the field the player spends most time in. For example, there are central defenders, and left and right midfielders. The ten outfield players may be arranged in these positions in any combination (for example, there may be four defenders, four midfielders, and two forwards, or three defenders, three midfielders, and four forwards), and the number of players in each position determines the style of the team's play; more forwards and fewer defenders would create a more aggressive and offensive-minded game, while the reverse would create a slower, more defensive style of play. While players may spend most of the game in a specific position, there are few restrictions on player movement, and players can switch positions at any time. The layout of the players on the pitch is called the team's *formation*, and defining the team's formation and tactics is usually the prerogative of the team's manager.

Development

Games revolving around the kicking of a ball have been played in many countries throughout history. According to FIFA, the "very earliest form of the game for which there is scientific evidence was an exercise of precisely this skilful technique dating back to the 2nd and 3rd centuries B.C. in China (the game of Cuju)." In addition, the Roman game *Harpastum* may be a distant ancestor of football. Various forms of football were played in medieval Europe, though rules varied greatly by both period and location.

Whilst football has continued to be played in various forms throughout the United Kingdom, the English public schools (fee-paying schools) are widely credited with certain key achievements in the creation of modern football (association football and the rugby football games — rugby league and rugby union football). During the sixteenth century English public schools generally, and headmaster Richard Mulcaster in particular, were instrumental in taking football away from its violent "mob" form and turning it into an organised team sport that was beneficial to schoolboys. Thereafter, the game became institutionalised, regulated, and part of a larger, more central tradition. Many early descriptions of football and references to it (e.g., in poetry) were recorded by people who had studied at these schools, showing they were familiar with the game. Finally, in the 19th century, teachers and former students were the first to write down formal rules of early modern football to enable matches to be played between schools.

The rules of football as they are codified today are based on the mid-19th century efforts to standardise the widely varying forms of football played at the public schools of England. The first ever set of football rules were written at Eton College in 1815. The Cambridge Rules were a code of football rules, first drawn up at Cambridge University in 1848, which have influenced the development of Association football and subsequent codes.

The Cambridge Rules were written at Trinity College, Cambridge in 1848, at a meeting attended by representatives from Eton, Harrow, Rugby, Winchester and Shrewsbury schools, but they were not universally adopted. During the 1850s, many clubs unconnected to schools or universities were formed throughout the English-speaking world to play various forms of football. Some came up with their own distinct codes of rules, most notably the Sheffield Football Club (formed by former pupils from Harrow) in 1857, which led to formation of a Sheffield FA in 1867. In 1862, John Charles Thring of Uppingham School also devised an influential set of rules.

These ongoing efforts contributed to the formation of The Football Association (The FA) in 1863 which first met on the morning of 26 October 1863 at the Freemason's Tavern in Great Queen Street, London. The only school to be represented on this occasion was Charterhouse. The Freemason's Tavern was the setting for five more meetings between October and December, which eventually produced the first comprehensive set of rules. At the final meeting, the first FA treasurer, the representative from Blackheath, withdrew his club from the FA over the removal of two draft rules at the previous meeting, the first which allowed for the running with the ball in hand and the second, obstructing such a run by hacking (kicking an opponent in the shins), tripping and holding.

Other English rugby football clubs followed this lead and did not join the FA, or subsequently left the FA and instead in 1871 formed the Rugby Football Union. The eleven remaining clubs, under the charge of Ebenezer Cobb Morley, went on to ratify the original thirteen laws of the game. These rules included handling of the ball by "marks" and the lack of a crossbar, rules which made it remarkably similar to Victorian rules football being developed at that time in Australia. The Sheffield FA played by its own rules until the 1870s with the FA absorbing some of its rules until there was little difference between the games.

The laws of the game are currently determined by the International Football Association Board (IFAB). The Board was formed in 1886 after a meeting in Manchester of The Football Association, the Scottish Football Association, the Football Association of Wales, and the Irish Football Association. The world's oldest football competition is the FA Cup, which was founded by C. W. Alcock and has been contested by English teams since 1872. The first official international football match took place in 1872 between Scotland and England in Glasgow, again at the instigation of C. W. Alcock. England is home to the world's first football league, which was founded in 1888 by Aston Villa director William McGregor. The original format contained 12 clubs from the Midlands and the North of England. The Fédération Internationale de Football Association (FIFA), the international football body, was formed in Paris in 1904 and declared that they would adhere to Laws of the Game of the Football Association.

The growing popularity of the international game led to the admittance of FIFA representatives to the International Football Association Board in 1913. The board currently consists of four representatives from FIFA and one representative from each of the four British associations.

Today, football is played at a professional level all over the world, and millions of people regularly go to football stadia to follow their favourite teams, whilst billions more watch the game on television. A very large number of people also play football at an amateur level. According to a survey conducted by FIFA and published in the spring of 2001, over 240 million people regularly play football in more than 200 countries in every part of the world. Its simple rules and minimal equipment requirements have no doubt aided its spread and growth in popularity.

In many parts of the world football evokes great passions and plays an important role in the life of individual fans, local communities, and even nations; it is therefore often claimed to be the most popular sport in the world. ESPN has spread the claim that the Côte d'Ivoire national football team helped secure a truce to the nation's civil war in 2005. By contrast, however, football is widely considered to be the final proximate cause in the Football War in June 1969 between El Salvador and Honduras. The sport also exacerbated tensions at the beginning of the Yugoslav wars of the 1990s, when a match between Dinamo Zagreb and Red Star Belgrade devolved into rioting in March 1990.

Laws of the Game

There are seventeen laws in the official Laws of the Game. The same Laws are designed to apply to all levels of football, although certain modifications for groups such as juniors, seniors or women are permitted. The laws are often framed in broad terms, which allow flexibility in their application depending on the nature of the game. In addition to the seventeen laws, numerous IFAB decisions and other directives contribute to the regulation of football. The laws can be found on the official FIFA website.

Players, Equipment and Officials

Each team consists of a maximum of eleven players (excluding substitutes), one of whom must be the goalkeeper. Competition rules may state a minimum number of players required to constitute a team; this is usually seven. Goalkeepers are the only players allowed to play the ball with their hands or arms, but they are only allowed to do so within the penalty area in front of their own goal. Though there are a variety of positions in which the outfield (non-goalkeeper) players are strategically placed by a coach, these positions are not defined or required by the Laws.

The basic equipment (kit) players are required to wear includes a shirt, shorts, socks, footwear and adequate shin guards. Players are forbidden to wear or use anything that is dangerous to themselves or another player (including jewellery or watches). The goalkeeper must wear clothing that is easily distinguishable from that worn by the other players and the match officials.

A number of players may be replaced by substitutes during the course of the game. The maximum number of substitutions permitted in most competitive international and domestic league games is three, though the number permitted may be varied in other leagues or in friendly matches. Common reasons for a substitution include injury, tiredness, ineffectiveness, a tactical switch, or as a defensive ploy to use up a little time at the end of a finely poised game. In standard adult matches, a player who has been substituted may not take further part in the match.

A game is officiated by a referee, who has "full authority to enforce the Laws of the Game in connection with the match to which he has been appointed" (Law 5), and whose decisions are final. The referee is assisted by two assistant referees. In many high-level games there is also a fourth official (and in the world cup a fifth official), who assist(s) the referee and may replace another official should the need arise.

Pitch

Due to the original formulation of the Laws in England and the early supremacy of the four British football associations within IFAB, the standard dimensions of a football pitch, or field, were originally expressed in imperial units. The Laws now express dimensions with approximate metric equivalents (followed by traditional units in brackets), though popular use tends to continue to use traditional units in English-speaking countries with a relatively recent history of metrification.

The length of the pitch specified for international adult matches is in the range 100-110 metres (110-120 yd) and the width is in the range 64-75 metres (70-80 yd). Fields for non-international matches may be 100-130 yards length and 50-100 yards in width, provided that the pitch does not become square. The longer boundary lines are *touchlines* or *sidelines*, while the shorter boundaries (on which the goals are placed) are *goal lines*. On the goal line at each end of the field a rectangular goal is centred. The inner edges of the vertical goal posts must be 8 yards (7.32 m) apart, and the lower edge of the horizontal crossbar supported by the goal posts must be 8 feet (2.44 m) above the ground. Nets are usually placed behind the goal, but are not required by the Laws.

In front of each goal is an area of the field known as the penalty area (colloquially "18-yard box" or simply "the box"). This area is marked by the goal-line, two lines starting on the goal-line 18 yards (16.5 m) from the goalposts and extending 18 yards into the pitch perpendicular to the goal-line, and a line joining them. This area has a number of functions, the most prominent being to mark where the goalkeeper may handle the ball and where a penal foul by a member of the defending team becomes punishable by a penalty kick. The field has various other markings and defined areas.

The Ball

A football is a ball used to play one of the different sports known as football. Each different code of football uses a different ball which belong to one of two different basic shapes:

— a sphere used in association football (soccer) as well as Gaelic football;

— a prolate spheroid, which may be either: those with more rounded ends used in rugby union, rugby league and Australian rules football

— the more pointed type used in American football and Canadian football

The ball used in football (soccer) is called a football (or soccer ball). Law 2 of the game specifies that the ball is an air-filled sphere with a circumference of 68–70 cm (or 27–28 inches), a weight of 410–450 g (or 14–16 ounces), inflated to a pressure of 60–110 kPa (or 8.5–15.6 psi), and covered in leather or "other suitable material". The weight specified for a ball is the dry weight: older balls often became significantly heavier in the course of a match played in wet weather. The standard ball is a Size 5. Smaller sizes exist; Size 3 is standard for team handball; others are used in underage games or as novelty items.

Most modern footballs are stitched from 32 panels of waterproofed leather or plastic: pigskin, 12 regular pentagons and 20 regular hexagons. The 32-panel configuration is similar to the polyhedron known as the truncated icosahedron, except that it is more spherical, because the faces bulge due to the pressure of the air inside. The first 32-panel ball was marketed by Select in the 1950s in Denmark. This configuration became common throughout Continental Europe in the 1960s, and was publicised worldwide by the Adidas Telstar, the official ball of the 1970 World Cup.

Older balls were usually stitched from 18 oblong non-waterproof leather panels, similar to the design of modern volleyballs and Gaelic footballs, and laced to allow access to the internal air bladder. This configuration is still common.

The official FIFA World Cup football for Germany 2006 matches was the 14-panel Adidas +Teamgeist. It was made in Thailand by Adidas, who have provided the official match balls for the tournament since 1970, and is a "thermally bonded" machine-pressed ball, rather than a traditionally stitched one. For future world cups, FIFA is hoping to alternate between Nike and Adidas for match balls. Another ball with an innovative pattern is the 26-panel Mitre PRO 100T.

There are also indoor footballs, which are made of one or two pieces of plastic. Often these have designs printed on them to resemble a stitched leather ball.

About 80% of association footballs are made in Pakistan. 75% of these (60% of all world production) are made in the city of Sialkot. In the past child labour was often used in the production of the balls. In 1996, during the European championship, activists decided to press this issue. This eventually led to the Atlanta Agreement, which forced ball manufacturers to make sure no child labour was involved in the fabrication of their products. This also led to a centralisation of production, which on the one hand would make it easier for the Independent Monitoring Association for Child Labour (IMAC) - an organization created to watch over the Atlanta Agreement - to make sure no child labour occurred, on the other hand often forced workers to commute further to get to work. Now the production takes place primarily in small workshops and factories and is now "totally free" of child labour.

In North America, the term football refers to a ball which is used to play American football or Canadian football. It is also referred to as a "pigskin". Nearly a prolate spheroid, it is slightly pointed at the ends, unlike the more elliptical rugby ball. The Canadian football is slightly less prolate than the American ball and has a closer resemblance to a rugby ball.The ball is about 11 inches (28 cm) long and about 22 inches (56 cm) in circumference at the center. The exterior of the ball is made of leather, which is required in professional and collegiate football. Footballs used in recreation may be made of rubber or plastic materials.

Leather panels are usually tanned to a natural brown color, which is usually required in professional leagues and collegiate play. At least one manufacturer uses leather that has been tanned to provide a "tacky" grip in dry or wet conditions.

The leather is usually stamped with a pebble-grain texture to help players grip the ball. Some or all of the panels may be stamped with the manufacturer's name, league or conference logos, signatures, and other markings.

Four panels or pieces of leather or plastic are required for each football. After a series of quality control inspections for weight and blemishes, workers begin the actual manufacturing process.

Two of the panels are perforated along adjoining edges, so that they can be laced together. One of these lacing panels receives an additional perforation and reinforcements in its center, to hold the inflation valve.

Each panel is attached to an interior lining. The four panels are then stitched together in an "inside-out" manner. The edges with the lacing holes, however, are not stitched together. The ball is then turned right side out by pushing the panels through the lacing hole.

A polyurethane or rubber lining called a bladder is then inserted through the lacing hole.

Polyvinyl chloride or leather laces are inserted through the perforations, to provide a grip for holding, hiking and passing the football.

Before play, the ball is inflated to an air pressure of 12.5–13.5 psi (86–93 kPa). The ball weighs 14–15 ounces (397–425 g).

According to nfl.com: The home club shall have 36 balls for outdoor games and 24 for indoor games available for testing with a pressure gauge by the referee two hours prior to the starting time of the game to meet with League requirements. Twelve new footballs, sealed in a special box and shipped by the manufacturer, will be opened in the officials' locker room two hours prior to the starting time of the game. These balls are to be specially marked with the letter "k" and used exclusively for the kicking game.

Regardless of the material used in manufacturing, the ball is sometimes colloquially referred to as a pigskin.

The football used in Australian football is similar to a rugby ball but generally slightly smaller and more rounded. A regulation football is 720–730 mm (28.3–28.7 in) in circumference, and 545–555 mm (21.5–21.9 in) transverse circumference, and inflated to a pressure of 62–76kPa (9–11 psi). In the AFL, the balls are red for day matches and yellow for night matches

Different sized and weight balls are used for different age levels, and for use with other sports such as Rec Footy and Women's Australian rules football.

Brands of balls used include Burley, Ross Faulkner, and the brand used in the Australian Football League, the Sherrin.

The Australian rules ball was invented by T.W. Sherrin in 1880, after he was given a misshapen rugby ball to fix. Sherrin designed the ball with indented rather than pointy ends to give the ball a better bounce. Before this time, a round ball was used from the 1850s to 1870s and later rugby balls were used to play the game.

Gaelic football is played with a spherical ball, roughly 25.4 cm (10 in) in diameter and 68.6 cm (27 in) to 73.7 cm (29 in) in circumference. A dry ball weighs between 370 g (13 oz) and 425 grams (15 oz). Gaelic footballs are also the standard balls used in International rules football.

Although Gaelic football has been played with a round ball since first organised in 1887, balls made by the Irish sports company O'Neills have been used sometime since the company was founded in 1918 and are recognised as the official ball to be played with, although it is now permitted to use the Gaelic ball manufactured by the Irish sports company Gaelic Gear.

Goal

The word goal refers to both the result of a score and the physical structure that defines where a score is achieved. A goal is scored after the ball passes completely over the goal line, between the goal posts and under the crossbar. Although the goal frame usually has a net attached to it, the net is simply to contain the ball when a goal is scored so that the referee can be certain the goal is legitimate, and the Laws of the Game do not strictly require the use of such a net. The exact definition of a goal is covered by law 10 of the Laws of the Game. A goalkeeper is the player of a team who is set into position to try to block shots into the goal.

In American and Canadian football, as well as Arena Football, a field goal is scored when a player either place kicks or drop kicks the ball from scrimmage through the plane bounded by the two uprights and above the crossbar. A set of goalposts is situated at each end of the field. Gridiron field goals count for three points, unless they are scored from a conversion. In Arena Football, drop kicked field goals count for four points, and drop kicked conversion goals count for two points.

In rugby union and rugby league, a field goal/drop goal or penalty goal refers to the same concept, but with slightly different scoring. All goals in rugby union count for 3 points except for conversions, which count for two. All goals in rugby league count for 2 points except for field goals, which count for 1.

In Australian rules football, a goal is scored when the ball contacts the foot of an attacker, touches no objects other than the ground, and entirely crosses the goal line between the two defensive goalposts. There is no cross-bar above which or below which the ball must pass. A goal is worth six points. If the ball touches any player on a part of their body other than their foot, hits a goal post, travels between a goal and a behind post, or is kicked by a defensive player into their own goal, only one point is scored.

In some countries, particularly Britain and Australia, the slang term woodwork is used to refer to the posts which constitute the structure of the goal. The term comes from the 19th century when the posts would be made of wood instead of iron or plastic as is more common today.

Goalkeeping

In many team sports, a goalkeeper is a designated player that is charged with directly preventing the opposite team from scoring by defending the goal. Such positions exist in hurling, association football, Gaelic football, International Rules Football, handball, field hockey, netball, water polo, lacrosse, floorball and a number of other sports. In ice hockey he or she is referred to most commonly as a goaltender or "netminder".

Usually special rules apply to the goalkeeper that do not apply to the other players. These rules are often instituted to protect the goalkeeper, being an obvious target for dangerous or even violent actions. In addition, in certain sports like ice hockey, goalkeepers are required to wear special equipment like heavy pads and a face mask to protect their bodies from impact from the play object (e.g. a puck). In soccer goalkeepers wear gloves that are protective to the hand because the fingers can be bent back.

In football, the goalkeeper occupies a position that represents the last line of defense between the opponent's offense and his own team's goal. The primary role of the goalkeeper is to defend his team's goal and prevent the opposition from scoring a goal. The goalkeeper is the only player who is permitted to touch the ball with his hands or arms in open play. Each team is required to have a goalkeeper on the field at all times during a match. If a goalkeeper is forced to leave the field due to injury or being sent off, another player must occupy the post, even if the team has no substitute goalkeeper available and/or has used up its allotted substitutions.

Goalkeeper is often abbreviated GK in lineup cards, match reports, and TV captions. The terms keeper and goalie are also commonly used. This position is colloquially referred as 'custodian' or 'the man between the posts'.

When assigning numbers to players on the team, if a squad number system is not in use, the number 1 shirt is usually reserved for the goalkeeper. Notable exceptions include Ubaldo Fillol, who wore the numbers 5 and 7 at the 1978 and 1982 FIFA World Cups.

Football, like many sports, has experienced many changes in tactics that have generated positions, as well as made positions disappear. Goalkeeper is the only position which is certain to have existed since the creation of the rules of the sport. Even in the early days of organized football, when systems were limited or non-existent and the main idea was for all field players to attack and defend, teams had a designated member to play as the goalkeeper.

The earliest account of football teams with player positions comes from Richard Mulcaster in 1581, however, he does not specify goalkeepers. The earliest specific reference to keeping goal comes from Cornish Hurling in 1602. According to Carew: "they pitch two bushes in the ground, some eight or ten foote asunder; and directly against them, ten or twelue score off, other twayne in like distance, which they terme their Goales. One of these is appoynted by lots, to the one side, and the other to his aduerse party. There is assigned for their gard, a couple of their best stopping Hurlers"

Other references to scoring goals begin in English literature in the early sixteenth century, for example in John Day's play The Blind Beggar of Bethnal Green (performed circa 1600; published 1659): "I'll play a gole at camp-ball" (an extremely violent variety of football, which was popular in East Anglia). Similarly in a poem in 1613, Michael Drayton refers to "when the Ball to throw, And drive it to the Gole, in squadrons forth they goe". It seems inevitable that wherever a game has evolved goals, some form of goalkeeping must also be developed. David Wedderburn refers to what has been translated from Latin as to "keep goal" in 1633 (however, contrary to media reports in 2006 he does not refer to the noun "goalkeeper". This is important as being a goalkeeper implies a fixed position throughout a match, whereas "keeping goal" suggests a temporary, fluid position accorded to whichever player or players find themselves nearest the goal. Wedderburn provides no evidence of such a fixed position on the field. It is not clear that what he meant by a goal was the same as modern usage; his word "metum" in the original Latin means the object to mark the end of a chariot race).

Initially, goalkeepers would typically play between the goalposts and had limited mobility, except when trying to save opposition shots. Throughout the years, goalkeeping has evolved, due to the changes on systems of play, to be a more active role. The original Laws of the Game permitted goalkeepers to handle the ball anywhere in their half of the pitch. This was revised in 1912, restricting use of the hands by the goalkeeper to the penalty area and goal box.

In the mid twentieth century, goalkeepers like Amadeo Carrizo pioneered a playing style that involved more mobility. He also helped introduce new techniques and strategies that would become a standard for the position. Carrizo was the first goalkeeper to wear gloves, the first one to leave the penalty area to defend his goal and the first one to use goal kicks as a strategy to start counter attack plays.

In 1992, the International Board made changes in the laws of the game that affected goalkeepers. Notably the back-pass rule, that prohibits goalkeepers from handling the ball with their hands when receiving a deliberate pass from a teammate that is not made with their head, shoulder, or chest. As a result, all goalkeepers were required to improve controlling the ball with their feet.

The goalkeeper position is the most specialized of all positions on the field. Unlike other players, goalkeepers may touch the ball with any part of their body except when they aren't in the penalty area where they are not allowed to use their hands and arms.

Although goalkeepers have special privileges under the laws of the game, they are otherwise subject to the same rules as any other player. Some goalkeepers,such as A.C Milan's Nelson Dida, are specialists at saving penalty kicks.

Goalkeepers are not required to stay in the penalty area. They may get involved in play anywhere on the pitch, and it is common for them to act as an additional defender during certain passages of the game. Colombia's René Higuita, Mexico's Jorge Campos and Liverpool's Bruce Grobbelaar were notable for their foot skills and their constant play outside the penalty area. Some goalkeepers have even scored goals; a number of goalkeepers have scored by rushing up to the opposite end of the pitch in order to create an advantage in numbers. This rush – nicknamed a "goalie run" – is risky, and is normally only done late in the game, in order to score a last-minute goal if the goalkeeper's team is losing (and only then, in situations where goal difference is unimportant). The action very rarely succeeds, although players like Michelangelo Rampulla, Jens Lehmann, Peter Schmeichel, Oscar Perez, Mart Poom, Marco Amelia, Andrés Palop, Brad Friedel, Massimo Taibi and Mark Crossley have been able to score in these situations.

In some even rarer situations, goalkeepers have even scored goals unintentionally, when a ball punted downfield has caught the opposing goalkeeper out of position. Paul Robinson and Pat Jennings have both scored under such circumstances, co-incidentally both doing so for Spurs.

Other goalkeepers have become notable at taking set pieces; for example, José Luis Chilavert, who is the only goalkeeper to score a hat trick (3 goals in a game), doing so through penalty kicks. He also was a free kick-expert. Rogério Ceni has scored the most amount goals for a goalkeeper, having scored 72 times (as of June 3, 2007) through free kicks and penalty kicks.

Goalkeepers must wear clothing that distinguishes them clearly from other players and match officials, as this is all that the FIFA Laws of the Game require. Some goalkeepers have received recognition for their match attire, like Lev Yashin who was nicknamed the "Black Panther" for his distinctive all-black outfit, or Jorge Campos, who was popular for his colorful attire. Goalkeepers kits are often a bright green or yellow.

Most goalkeepers also wear goalkeeper gloves to improve their grip on the ball, and to protect themselves from injury. There are now gloves that have features designed to prevent injuries such as sprained fingers. Gloves are not mandatory, however due to the increased grip they give it is very rare for a goalkeeper to play without them in professional matches. They may be removed for penalty shoot-outs though.

The most expensive goalkeeper ever to be bought by a British club was Craig Gordon, who signed for Sunderland A.F.C. from Scottish club Heart of Midlothian on the 7th August 2007 for £9m. He is also the third most expensive of all time after Gianluigi Buffon (£30 million to Juventus from Parma) and Antonio Peruzzi (£10.5 million from Juventus to Internazionale).

The first reported use of goalkeeping gloves was in 1952 in an Airdrie vs Celtic game. Before the 1960s it was uncommon for goalkeepers to wear gloves except under very poor weather conditions when they were just used for warmth. The use of gloves designed for grip steadily became more popular into the 1980s by which time most professionals had adopted the use of gloves. In the late 1990s gloves offering hyperextension protection became available and soon had become a very mainstream product.

On the sporting field, goalposts are posts between which players must carry, kick or pass a ball or similar object in order to score points, or simply a goal. In many games, at each end of the field of play, there are two vertical posts (or uprights) supporting a horizontal crossbar. In some games, such as Association Football or

Hockey, the object is to pass the ball between the posts below the crossbar, while in others, such as those based on Rugby, the ball must pass over the crossbar instead. In Gaelic Football, in which the goalposts are similar to those used in rugby, the ball can be kicked either under the crossbar for a goal, or over the crossbar through the posts for a point. There are other variants too. In Australian Rules Football, there is no crossbar but 4 uprights instead. In Netball, a single post at each end of the court supports a horizontal hoop that the ball must fall through. While in Basketball, where the hoop and associated backboard was originally supported on a post, the posts themselves have been done away in most cases, with and the hoop and backboard now being suspended over the court from a stadium wall or ceiling.

Duration and Tie-breaking

A standard adult football match consists of two periods of 45 minutes each, known as halves. Each half runs continuously, meaning that the clock is not stopped when the ball is out of play; the referee does, however, make allowance for time lost through significant stoppages as described below. There is usually a 15-minute "half-time" break between halves. The end of the match is known as full-time.

The referee is the official timekeeper for the match, and may make an allowance for time lost through substitutions, injured players requiring attention, or other stoppages. This added time is commonly referred to as *stoppage time* or *injury time*, and is at the sole discretion of the referee. The referee alone signals the end of the match. In matches where a fourth official is appointed, toward the end of the half the referee signals how many minutes of stoppage time he intends to add, and the fourth official then informs the players and spectators by holding up a board showing this number. The signalled stoppage time may be further extended by the referee.

In league competitions games may end in a draw, but in some knockout competitions if a game is tied at the end of regulation time it may go into extra time, which consists of two further 15-minute periods. If the score is still tied after extra time, some competitions allow the use of penalty shootouts (known officially in the Laws of the Game as "kicks from the penalty mark") to determine which team will progress to the next stage of the tournament. Goals scored during extra time periods count toward the final score of the game, but kicks from the penalty mark are only used to decide the team that progresses to the next part of the tournament (with goals scored in a penalty shootout not making up part of the final score).

Competitions held over two legs (in which each team plays at home once) may use the away goals rule to attempt to determine which team progresses in the event of equal aggregate scores. If the result is still equal following this calculation kicks from the penalty mark are usually required, though some competitions may require a tied game to be replayed.

In the late 1990s, the IFAB experimented with ways of making matches more likely to end without requiring a penalty shootout, which was often seen as an undesirable way to end a match. These involved rules ending a game in extra time early, either when the first goal in extra time was scored (golden goal), or if one team held a lead at the end of the first period of extra time (silver goal). Golden goal was used at the World Cup in 1998 (France) and 2002 (Japan-South Korea). The first World Cup game decided by a golden goal was France's victory over Paraguay in 1998. In Euro 1996, Germany was the first nation to score a golden goal in a major competition, beating Czech Republic in the final. Silver goal was used in Euro 2004 (Portugal). Both these experiments have been discontinued by IFAB.

Ball in and Out of Play

Under the Laws, the two basic states of play during a game are *ball in play* and *ball out of play*. From the beginning of each playing period with a kick-off (a set kick from the centre-spot by one team) until the end of the playing period, the ball is in play at all times, except when either the ball leaves the field of play, or play is stopped by the referee. When the ball becomes out of play, play is restarted by one of eight restart methods depending on how it went out of play:

— *Kick-off:* following a goal by the opposing team, or to begin each period of play.

— *Throw-in:* when the ball has wholly crossed the touchline; awarded to opposing team to that which last touched the ball.

— *Goal kick:* when the ball has wholly crossed the goal line without a goal having been scored and having last been touched by an attacker; awarded to defending team.

— *Corner kick:* when the ball has wholly crossed the goal line without a goal having been scored and having last been touched by a defender; awarded to attacking team.

— *Indirect free kick:* awarded to the opposing team following "non-penal" fouls, certain technical infringements, or when play is stopped to caution/send-off an opponent without a specific foul having occurred. A goal may not be scored directly from an indirect free kick.

— *Direct free kick:* awarded to fouled team following certain listed "penal" fouls.

— *Penalty kick*: awarded to the fouled team following a foul usually punishable by a direct free kick but that has occurred within their opponent's penalty area.

— *Dropped-ball*: occurs when the referee has stopped play for any other reason (e.g., a serious injury to a player, interference by an external party, or a ball becoming defective). This restart is uncommon in adult games.

FOULS AND MISCONDUCT

A foul occurs when a player commits a specific offence listed in the Laws of the Game when the ball is in play. The offences that constitute a foul are listed in Law 12. Handling the ball deliberately, tripping an opponent, or pushing an opponent, are examples of "penal fouls", punishable by a direct free kick or penalty kick depending on where the offence occurred. Other fouls are punishable by an indirect free kick.

The referee may punish a player or substitute's misconduct by a caution (yellow card) or sending-off (red card). A second yellow card at the same game leads to a red card, and therefore to a sending-off. Misconduct may occur at any time, and while the offences that constitute misconduct are listed, the definitions are broad. In particular, the offence of "unsporting behaviour" may be used to deal with most events that violate the spirit of the game, even if they are not listed as specific offences. Non-players, such as managers and support staff, may be dismissed from the field and its surrounds by the referee if they fail to conduct themselves in a responsible manner.

Rather than stopping play, the referee may allow play to continue when its continuation will benefit the team against which an offence has been committed. This is known as "playing an advantage". The referee may "call back" play and penalise the original offence if the anticipated advantage does not ensue within a short period of time, typically taken to be four to five seconds. Even if an offence is not penalised because the referee plays an advantage, the offender may still be sanctioned for any associated misconduct at the next stoppage of play.

The offside law effectively limits the ability of attacking players to remain forward (i.e. closer to the opponent's goal-line) of the ball, the second-to-last defending player (which can include the goalkeeper), and the half-way line.

Governing Bodies

The recognised international governing body of football (and associated games, such as futsal and beach soccer) is the Fédération Internationale de Football Association (FIFA). The FIFA headquarters are located in Zürich, Switzerland.

Six regional confederations are associated with FIFA; these are:

— *Asia:* Asian Football Confederation (AFC)

— *Africa:* Confederation of African Football (CAF)

— *Central/North America & Caribbean:* Confederation of North, Central American and Caribbean Association Football (CONCACAF; also known as The Football Confederation)

— *Europe:* Union of European Football Associations (UEFA)

— *Oceania*: Oceania Football Confederation (OFC)

— *South America*: Confederación Sudamericana de Fútbol (South American Football Confederation; CONMEBOL)

The recognised various national associations oversee football within their jurisdictions. These are affiliated both with FIFA directly and also with their respective continental confederations. The Laws of the Game are not maintained by FIFA itself; rather they are maintained by the International Football Association Board.

Major International Competitions

The major international competition in football is the World Cup, organised by FIFA. This competition takes place over a four-year period. More than 190 national teams compete in qualifying tournaments within the scope of continental confederations for a place in the finals. The finals tournament, which is held every four years, now involves 32 national teams (increased in 1998 from the 24 of 1994) competing over a four-week period. The 2006 FIFA World Cup took place in Germany; in 2010 it will be held in South Africa.

There has been a football tournament at every Summer Olympic Games since 1900, except at the 1932 games in Los Angeles. Prior to the inception of the World Cup, the Olympics (especially during the 1920s) had the same status as the World Cup. Originally, the event was for amateurs only, however, since the 1984 Summer Olympics professionals have been permitted as well, albeit with certain restrictions which effectively prevent countries from fielding their strongest sides. Currently, the Olympic men's tournament is played at Under-23 level. In the past the Olympics have allowed a restricted number of over-age players per team; but that practice will cease in the 2008 Olympics.

The Olympic competition is not generally considered to carry the same international significance and prestige as the World Cup. A women's tournament was added in 1996; in contrast to the men's event, the women's

Olympic tournament is played by full international sides without age restrictions. It thus carries international prestige considered comparable to that of the FIFA Women's World Cup.

After the World Cup, the most important football competitions are the continental championships, which are organised by each continental confederation and contested between national teams. These are the European Championship (UEFA), the Copa América (CONMEBOL), African Cup of Nations (CAF), the Asian Cup (AFC), the CONCACAF Gold Cup (CONCACAF) and the OFC Nations Cup (OFC). Two of the most prestigious competitions in club football are the respective continental championships, which are generally contested between national champions, for example the UEFA Champions League in Europe and the Copa Libertadores de América in South America. The most prestigious competition until 2005 was the Intercontinental Cup which was contested by the winner club of the European Champions League cup and the winner of the Copa Libertadores. This was a single match played in Tokyo, Japan and went from 1980 until 2004. This was also known as the Toyota Cup. Due to the growing number of audience and interest of people from Africa, North America and Asia, this "cup" was replaced in 2005 by the FIFA Club World Cup in which there is no single match, but a whole tournament between the winners of the six club championships of each FIFA confederation.

Domestic Competitions

The governing bodies in each country operate league systems, normally comprising several divisions, in which the teams gain points throughout the season depending on results. Teams are placed into tables, placing them in order according to points accrued. Most commonly, each team plays every other team in its league at home and away in each season, in a round-robin tournament. At the end of a season, the top team are declared to be the champions, and the top few teams may be promoted to a higher division; and one or more of the teams finishing at the bottom are relegated to a lower division. The teams finishing at the top of a country's league may be eligible also to play in international club competitions in the following season. The main exceptions to this system occur in some Latin American leagues, which divide football championships into two sections named Apertura and Clausura, awarding a champion for each.

In addition to a league system, most countries operate one or more *cup* competitions during the season. These are organised on a knock-out basis, the winner of each match proceeding to the next round; the loser takes no further part in the competition.

2

History of Football

The contemporary history of football spans more than 100 years. It all began in 1863 in England, when rugby football and association football branched off on their different courses and the world's first football association was founded - The Football Association in England. Both forms of football stemmed from a common root and both have a long and intricately branched ancestral tree. Their early history reveals at least half a dozen different games, varying to different degrees and to which the historical development of football is related and has actually been traced back. Whether this can be justified in some instances is disputable. Nevertheless, the fact remains that playing a ball with the feet has been going on for thousands of years and there is absolutely no reason to believe that it is an aberration of the more "natural" form of playing a ball with the hands.

On the contrary, apart from the absolute necessity to employ the legs and feet in such a tough bodily tussle for the ball, often without any laws for protection, it was no doubt recognised right at the outset that the art of controlling the ball with the feet was extremely difficult and, as such, it required special technique and talent. The very earliest form of the game for which there is scientific evidence was an exercise of precisely this skilful technique dating back to the 2nd and 3rd centuries B.C.

in China. A military manual dating from the period of the Han Dynasty includes among the physical education exercises, the "Tsu'Chu". This consisted of kicking a leather ball filled with feathers and hair through an opening, measuring only 30 - 40 cm in width, into a small net fixed onto long bamboo canes - a feat which obviously demanded great skill and excellent technique. A variation of this exercise also existed, whereby the player was not permitted to aim at his target unimpeded, but had to use his feet, chest, back and shoulders whilst trying to withstand the attacks of his opponents. Use of the hands was not permitted. The ball artistry of today's top players is therefore not quite as new as some people may assume.

Another form of the game, also originating from the Far East, was the Japanese Kemari, which dates from about 500 to 600 years later and is still played today. This is a type of circular football game, far less spectacular, but, for that reason, a 'more dignified and ceremonious experience, requiring certain skills, but not competitive ' in the way the Chinese game was, nor is there the slightest sign of struggle for possession of the ball. The players had to pass the ball to each other, in a relatively small space, trying not to let it touch the ground.

The Greek game "episkyros", relatively little of which has been handed down, was much livelier, as was the Roman game "Harpastum". The latter was played with a smaller ball with two teams contesting the game on a rectangular field marked by boundary lines and a centre-line. The object was to get the ball over the opponents' boundary lines. The ball was passed between players and trickery was the order of the day. Each team member had his own specific tactical assignment and the spectators took a vociferous interest in the proceedings and the score. The role of the feet in this game was so small as scarcely to be of consequence. This game remained popular for 700 or 800 years, but, although the Romans took it to England with them, it is doubtful whether it can be considered as a forerunner of contemporary football. The same applies for hurling, a popular game with the Celtic population, which is played to this very day in Cornwall and Ireland. It is possible that influences were asserted, but it is certain that the decisive development of the game of football with which we are now familiar took place in England and Scotland.

The game that flourished in the British Isles from the 8th to the 19th centuries had a considerable variety of local and regional versions - which were subsequently smoothed down and smartened up to form the present day sports of association football and rugby football. - They were substantially different from all the previously known forms - more disorganised, more violent, more spontaneous and usually played by an indefinite number of players. Frequently, the games took the form of a heated contest between whole village communities or townships - through streets, village squares, across fields, hedges, fences and streams. Kicking was allowed, as in fact was almost everything else. However, in some of these games kicking was out of the question due to the size and weight of the ball being used. In such cases, kicking was instead employed to fell opponents. Incidentally, it was not until nine years after the football rules had been established for the first time in 1863 that the size and weight of the ball were finally standardised. Up to that time, agreement on this point had usually been reached by the parties concerned when they were arranging the match, as was the case for the game between London and Sheffield in 1866. This match was also the first where the duration of the game was prearranged for one and a half hours.

Shrovetide football, as it was called, belonged in the "mob football" category, where the number of players was unlimited and the rules were fairly vague (for example, according to an ancient handbook from Workington in England, any means could be employed to get the ball to its target with the exception of murder and manslaughter). Shrovetide football is still played today on Shrove Tuesday in some areas, for example, Ashbourne in Derbyshire. Needless to say, it is no longer so riotous as it used to be, nor are such extensive casualties suffered as was probably the case centuries ago.

This game is reputedly Anglo-Saxon in origin and there are many legends concerning its first appearance. For example, in both Kingston-on-Thames and Chester, the story goes that the game was played for the very first time with the severed head of a vanquished Danish prince. In Derby, it is said to have originated far earlier, in the 3rd century, during the victory celebrations that followed a battle against the Romans.

Despite the legends of Kingston and Chester, certain facts appear to contradict the Anglo-Saxon theory. Namely that there is no evidence of it having been played at this time in Saxon areas or on the continent, nor is the game mentioned in early Anglo-Saxon literature. Prior to the Norman Conquest, the only trace found of any such ball game comes from a Celtic source.

One other possible theory regarding its origin is that when the aforementioned "mob football" was being played in the British Isles in the early centuries A.D., a very similar game was thriving in France, particularly in Normandy and Brittany. So it is quite feasible that the Normans brought this form of the game to England with them.

All these theories produce a picture quite bewildering in its complexity - far more complex than the simple rules that governed this form of the game, if we dare even to call them rules.

Quite apart from man's natural impulse to demonstrate his strength and skill, even in this chaotic and turbulent fashion, it is certain that in many cases, pagan customs, especially fertility rites, played a major role. The ball symbolised the sun, which had to be conquered in order to secure a bountiful harvest. The ball had to be propelled around, or across, a field so that the crops would flourish and the attacks of the opponents had to be warded off.

A similar significance was attached to the games between married men and bachelors that prevailed for centuries in some parts of England, and, likewise, to the famous game between married and unmarried women in the Scottish town of Inveresk at the end of the 17th century which, perhaps by design, was regularly won by the married women. Women's football is obviously not so new as some people think.

Scholars might have conflicting views on the origins of the game and the influences that certain cults may have had on its evolution, but one thing is incontestable: football has flourished for over a thousand years in diverse rudimentary forms, in the very region which we describe as its home, England and the British Isles. The chain of prohibitions and censures, sometimes harsh, sometimes mild, proves beyond a shadow of a doubt what tremendous enthusiasm there was for football, even though it was so often frowned upon by the authorities. The repeated unsuccessful intervention of the authorities and high offices of the land shows how powerless they were to restrict it, in spite of their condemnation and threats of severe punishment.

As long ago as 1314 the Lord Mayor of London saw fit to issue a proclamation forbidding football within the city due to the rumpus it usually caused. Infringement of this law meant imprisonment. King Edward III passed extremely harsh measures in 1331 to suppress football, which was regarded as a public nuisance. At the same time, similar measures were also introduced in France.

During the 100 years' war between England and France from 1338 to 1453 the court was also unfavourably disposed towards football, albeit for different reasons. Edward III, Richard II, Henry IV and Henry V made football punishable by law because the well-loved recreation prevented their subjects from practising more useful military disciplines, particularly archery, which played an important and valuable role in the English army at that time.

All the Scottish kings of the 15th Century also deemed it necessary to censure and prohibit football. Particularly famous amongst these was the decree proclaimed by the Parliament convened by James I in 1424: "That na man play at the Fute-ball". None of these efforts had much effect. The popularity of the game amongst the people and their obvious delight in the rough and tumble for the ball went far too deep to be uprooted.

The passion for football was particularly exuberant in Elizabethan times. An influence that most likely played a part in intensifying the native popularity for the game came from Renaissance Italy, particularly from Florence, but also from Venice and other cities that had produced their own brand of football known as "Calcio". It was certainly more organised than the English equivalent and was played by teams dressed in coloured livery at the important gala events held on certain holidays in Florence. It was a truly splendid spectacle. In England the game was still as rough and ungracious and lacking in refinement as ever, but it did at this time find a prominent supporter who commended if for other reasons when he saw the simple joy of the players romping after the ball. This supporter was Richard

Mulcaster, the great pedagogue, head of the famous schools of Merchant Taylor's and St. Paul's. He pointed out that the game had positive educational value and it promoted health and strength. He claimed that all that was needed was to refine it a little and give it better manners. His notion was that the game would benefit most if the number of participants in each team were limited and, more importantly, there were a stricter referee.

Resentment of football up to this time had been mainly for practical reasons. The game had been regarded as a public disturbance that resulted in damage to property, for example, in Manchester in 1608, football was banned again because so many windows had been smashed.

In the course of the 16th century a quite new type of attack was launched against football. With the spread of Puritanism, the cry went up against "frivolous" amusements, and sport happened to be classified as such, football in particular. The main objection was that it supposedly constituted a violation of peace on the Sabbath. Similar attacks were made against the theatre, which strait-laced Puritans regarded as a source of idleness and iniquity. This laid the foundations for the entertainment ban on English Sundays, which would later become a permanent feature during the Commonwealth and Puritanical eras (even though it is said that Oliver Cromwell himself was a keen footballer in his youth). From then on football on Sundays was taboo. It remained so for some 300 years, until the ban was lifted once again, at first unofficially and ultimately with the formal consent of The Football Association, albeit on a rather small scale.

However, none of these obstacles could eradicate football. Take Derby as an example. Between 1731 and 1841, the town's authorities made continual attempts to ban football from the streets. In the end, they had to resort to riot laws before there was any effect at all.

All told there was scarcely any progress at all in the development of football for hundreds of years. But, although the game was persistently forbidden for 500 years, it was never completely suppressed. As a consequence, it remained essentially rough, violent and disorganised. A change did not come about until the beginning of the 19th century when school football became the custom, particularly in the famous public schools. This was the turning point. In this new environment, it was possible to make innovations and refinements to the game.

The rules were still relatively free and easy as there was still no standard, organised form of the game. Each school in fact developed its own adaptation and, at times, these varied considerably. The traditional aspects of the game remained but innovations depended for the most part on the playing ground available. If use had to be made of a paved school playground, surrounded by a brick wall, then there was simply not enough space for the old hurly-burly mob football. Circumstances such as these made schools like Charterhouse, Westminster, Eton and Harrow give birth to the type of game in which more depended on the players' dribbling virtuosity than the robust energy required in a scrum. On the other hand, schools such as Cheltenham and Rugby were more inclined towards the more rugged game in which the ball could be touched with the hands or even carried. All these early styles were given a great boost when it was recognised in educational circles that football was not merely an excuse to indulge in a childish romp, but could actually be beneficial educationally. What is more it was accepted that it also constituted a useful distraction from less desirable occupations, such as heavy drinking and gambling. A new attitude began to permeate the game, eventually leading to a "games cult" in public schools. This materialised when it was observed how well the team game served to encourage such fine qualities as loyalty, selflessness, cooperation, subordination and deference to the team spirit. Games became an integral part of the school curriculum and participation in football became compulsory. Dr. Thomas Arnold, the head of Rugby school, made further advances in this direction, when in 1846 in Rugby the first truly standardised rules for an organised game were laid down. These were in any event quite rough enough, for example, they permitted kicking an opponent's legs below the knees, with the reserve that he should not be held still whilst his shins were being worked on. Handling the ball was also allowed and ever since the memorable occasion in 1823 when William Webb Ellis, to the amazement of his own team and his opponents, made a run with the ball tucked under his arm, carrying the ball has been permitted. Many schools followed suit and adopted the rules laid down in Rugby, others, such as Eton, Harrow and Winchester, rejected this form of football, and gave preference to kicking the ball and carrying it was forbidden. Charterhouse and Westminster were also against handling the ball. However, they did not isolate their style as some schools did, instead they formed a nucleus from which this style of game began to spread.

Finally, in 1863, developments reached a climax. At Cambridge University, where in 1848 attempts had already been made by former pupils from the various schools to find a common denominator for all the different adaptations of the game, a fresh initiative began to establish some uniform standards and rules that would be accepted by everyone. It was at this point that the majority spoke out against such rough customs as tripping, shin-kicking and so on. As it happened, the majority also expressed disapproval at carrying the ball. It was this that caused the Rugby group to withdraw. They would probably have agreed to refrain from shin-kicking, which was in fact later banned in the Rugby regulations, but they were reluctant to relinquish carrying the ball.

This Cambridge action was an endeavour to sort out the utter confusion surrounding the rules. The decisive initiative, however, was taken after a series of meetings organised at the end of the same year (1863) in London. On 26 October 1863, eleven London clubs and schools sent their representatives to the Freemason's Tavern. These representatives were intent on clarifying the muddle by establishing a set of fundamental rules, acceptable to all parties, to govern the matches played amongst them. This meeting marked the birth of The Football Association. The eternal dispute concerning shin-kicking, tripping and carrying the ball was discussed thoroughly at this and consecutive meetings until eventually on 8 December the die-hard exponents of the Rugby style took their final leave. They were in the minority anyway. They wanted no part in a game that forbade tripping, shin-kicking and carrying the ball. A stage had been reached where the ideals were no longer compatible. On 8 December 1863, football and rugby finally split. Their separation became totally irreconcilable six years hence when a provision was included in the football rules forbidding any handling of the ball (not only carrying it).

Only eight years after its foundation, The Football Association already had 50 member clubs. The first football competition in the world was started in the same year - the FA Cup, which preceded the League Championship by 17 years.

International matches were being staged in Great Britain before football had hardly been heard of in Europe. The first was played in 1872 and was contested by England and Scotland. This sudden boom of organised football accompanied by staggering crowds of spectators brought with it certain problems with which other countries were not confronted until much later on. Professionalism was one of them. The first moves in this direction came in 1879, when Darwin, a small Lancashire club, twice managed to draw against the supposedly invincible Old Etonians in the FA Cup, before the famous team of London amateurs finally scraped through to win at the third attempt. Two Darwin players, the Scots John Love and Fergus Suter, are reported as being the first players ever to receive remuneration for their football talent. This practice grew rapidly and the Football Association found itself obliged to legalise professionalism as early as 1885. This development predated the formation of any national association outside of Great Britain (namely, in the Netherlands and Denmark) by exactly four years.

After the English Football Association, the next oldest are the Scottish FA (1873), the FA of Wales (1875) and the Irish FA (1880). Strictly speaking, at the time of the first international match, England had no other partner association against which to play. When Scotland played England in Glasgow on 30 November 1872, the Scottish FA did not even exist - it was not founded for another three months. The team England played that day was actually the oldest Scottish club team, Queen's Park.

The spread of football outside of Great Britain, mainly due to the British influence abroad, started slow, but it soon gathered momentum and spread rapidly to all parts of the world. The next countries to form football associations after the Netherlands and Denmark in 1889 were New Zealand (1891), Argentina (1893), Chile (1895), Switzerland, Belgium (1895), Italy (1898), Germany, Uruguay (both in 1900), Hungary (1901) and Finland (1907). When FIFA was founded in Paris in May 1904 it had seven founder members: France, Belgium, Denmark, the Netherlands, Spain (represented by the Madrid FC), Sweden and Switzerland. The German Football Federation cabled its intention to join on the same day.

This international football community grew steadily, although it sometimes met with obstacles and setbacks. In 1912, 21 national associations were already affiliated to the Fédération Internationale de Football Association (FIFA). By 1925, the number had increased to 36, in 1930 - the year of the first World Cup - it was 41, in 1938, 51 and in 1950, after the interval caused by the Second World War, the number had reached 73. At present, after the 2000 Ordinary FIFA Congress, FIFA has 204 members in every part of the world.

3

Laws of Football

Law 1 - The Field of Play

Field Surface

— Matches may be played on natural or artificial surfaces, according to the rules of the competition.

Dimensions

— The field of play must be rectangular. The length of the touch line must be greater than the length of the goal line.

minimum	maximum	
Length:	90 m (100 yds)	120 m (130 yds)
Width:	45 m (50 yds)	90 m (100 yds)

International Matches

minimum	maximum	
Length:	100 m (110 yds)	110 m (120 yds)
Width:	64 m (70 yds)	75 m (80 yds)

Field Markings

— The field of play is marked with lines. These lines belong to the areas of which they are boundaries.

— The two longer boundary lines are called touch lines. The two shorter lines are called goal lines.

— All lines are not more than 12 cm (5 ins) wide.

— The field of play is divided into two halves by a halfway line.

— The centre mark is indicated at the midpoint of the halfway line.

— A circle with a radius of 9.15 m (10 yds) is marked around it.

The Goal Area

A goal area is defined at each end of the field as follows:

— Two lines are drawn at right angles to the goal line, 5.5 m (6 yds) from the inside of each goalpost. These lines extend into the field of play for a distance of 5.5 m (6 yds) and are joined by a line drawn parallel with the goal line.

— The area bounded by these lines and the goal line is the goal area.

The Penalty Area

— A penalty area is defined at each end of the field as follows:

  — Two lines are drawn at right angles to the goal line, 16.5 m (18 yds) from the inside of each goalpost. These lines extend into the field of play for a distance of 16.5 m (18 yds) and are joined by a line drawn parallel with the goal line. The area bounded by these lines and the goal line is the penalty area.

  — Within each penalty area, a penalty mark is made 11 m (12 yds) from the midpoint between the goalposts and equidistant to them. An arc of a circle with a radius of 9.15 m (10 yds) from each penalty mark is drawn outside the penalty area.

Flagposts

— A flagpost, not less than 1.5 m (5 ft) high, with a non-pointed top and a flag is placed at each corner.

— Flagposts may also be placed at each end of the halfway line, not less than 1 m (1 yd) outside the touch line.

The Corner Arc

— A quarter circle with a radius of 1 m (1 yd) from each corner flagpost is drawn inside the field of play.

Goals

— Goals must be placed on the centre of each goal line.

— They consist of two upright posts equidistant from the corner flagposts and joined at the top by a horizontal crossbar.

— The distance between the posts is 7.32 m (8 yds) and the distance from the lower edge of the crossbar to the ground is 2.44 m (8 ft).

— Both goalposts and the crossbar have the same width and depth, which do not exceed 12 cm (5 ins). The goal lines are the same width as that of the goalposts and the crossbar. Nets may be attached to the goals and the ground behind the goal, provided that they are properly supported and do not interfere with the goalkeeper.

— The goalposts and crossbars must be white as shown below:

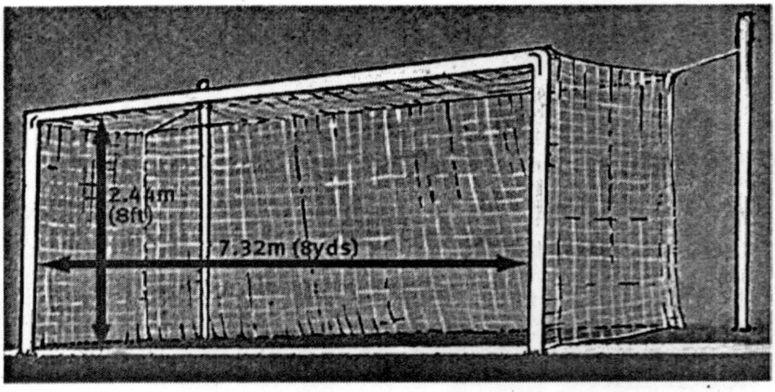

Safety

— Goals must be anchored securely to the ground. Portable goals may only be used if they satisfy this requirement.

The Field of Play

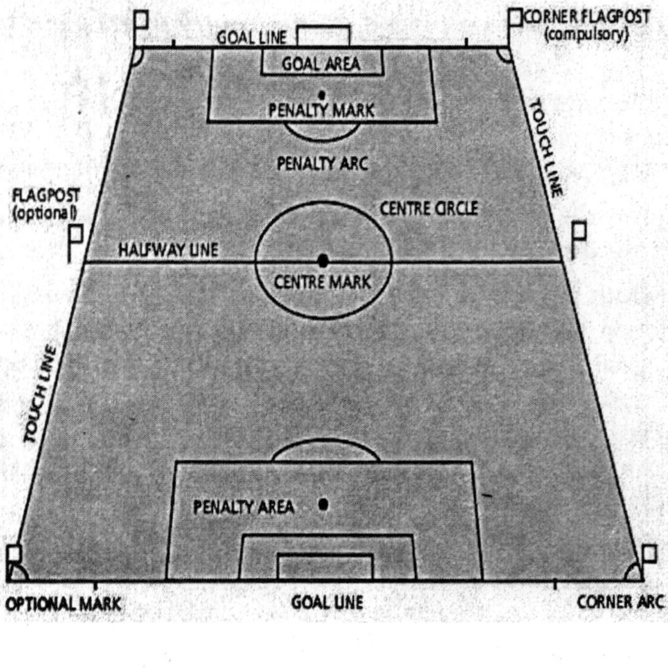

Corner Flagpost

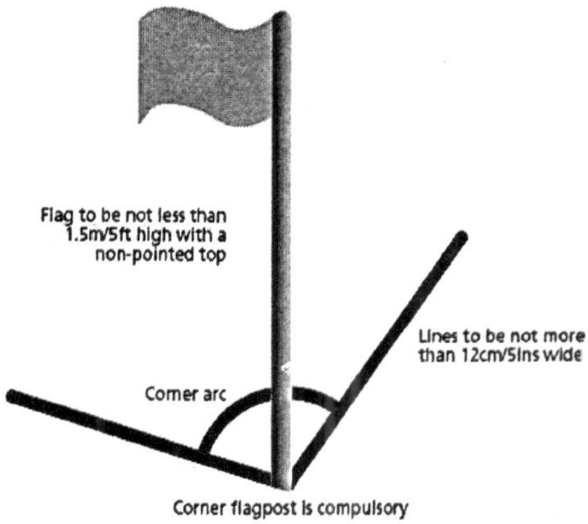

Metric Measurements

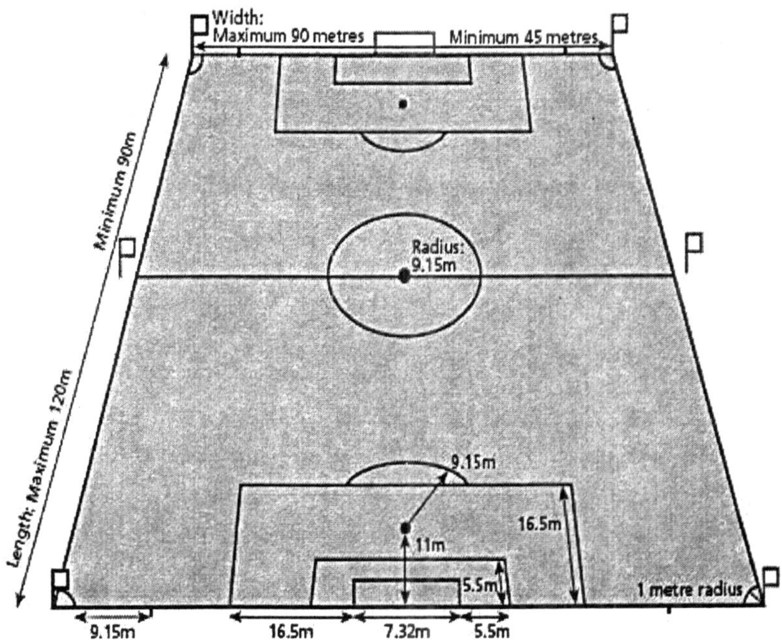

Imperial Measurements

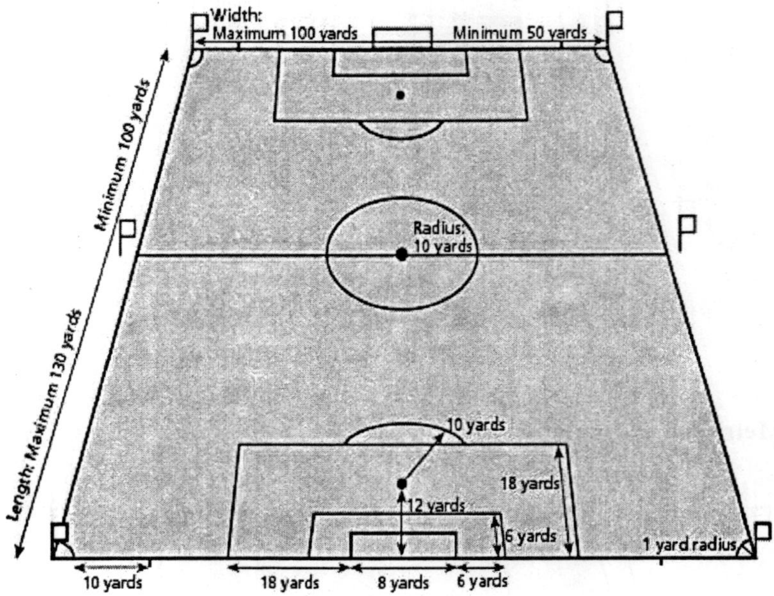

Decisions of the International F.A. Board

— *Decision 1*: If the crossbar becomes displaced or broken, play is stopped until it has been repaired or replaced in position. If a repair is not possible, the match is abandoned. The use of a rope to replace the crossbar is not permitted. If the crossbar can be repaired, the match is restarted with a dropped ball at the place where the ball was located when play was stopped.

— *Decision 2*: Goalposts and crossbars must be made of wood, metal or other approved material. Their shape may be square, rectangular, round or elliptical and they must not be dangerous to players.

— *Decision 3*: No kind of commercial advertising, whether real or virtual, is permitted on the field of play and field equipment (including the goal nets and the areas they enclose) from the time the teams enter the field of play until they have left it at half-time and from the time the teams re-enter the field of play until the end of the match. In particular, no advertising material of any kind may be displayed on goals, nets, flagposts or their flags. No extraneous equipment (cameras, microphones, etc.) may be attached to these items.

— *Decision 4*: There shall be no advertising of any kind within the technical area or within one metre of the touch line and outside the field of play on the ground. Further, no advertising shall be allowed in the area between the goal line and the goal nets.

— *Decision 5*: The reproduction, whether real or virtual, of representative logos or emblems of FIFA, confederations, member associations, leagues, clubs or other bodies is forbidden on the field of play and field equipment (including the goal nets and the areas they enclose) during playing time, as described in Decision 3.

— *Decision 6*: A mark may be made off the field of play, 9.15 metres (10 yds) from the corner arc and at right angles to the goal lines, to ensure that this distance is observed when a corner kick is being taken.

— *Decision 7*: Where artificial surfaces are used in either competition matches between representative teams of member associations affiliated to FIFA or international club competition matches, the surface must meet the requirements of the FIFA Quality Concept for Artificial Turf or the International Artificial Turf Standard, unless special dispensation is given by FIFA.

— *Decision 8*: Where a technical area exists, it must meet the requirements approved by the International F.A. Board.

Law 2 – The Ball

Qualities and Measurements

The ball is:

— spherical;

— made of leather or other suitable material;

— of a circumference of not more than 70 cm (28 ins) and not lessthan 68 cm (27 ins);

— not more than 450 g (16 oz) in weight and not less than 410 g (14 oz) at the start of the match;

— of a pressure equal to 0.6 – 1.1 atmosphere (600 – 1100 g/cm^2) at sea level (8.5 lbs/sq in – 15.6 lbs/sq in).

Replacement of a Defective Ball

If the ball bursts or becomes defective during the course of a match:

— the match is stopped;

— the match is restarted by dropping the replacement ball at the place where the first ball became defective.

If the ball bursts or becomes defective whilst not in play at a kick-off, goal kick, corner kick, free kick, penalty kick or throw-in:

— the match is restarted accordingly.

Replacement of a Defective Ball

The ball may not be changed during the match without the authority of the referee.

Decisions of the International F.A. Board

Decision 1

In competition matches, only footballs that meet the minimum technical requirements stipulated in Law 2 are permitted for use.

In FIFA competition matches, and in competition matches organised under the auspices of the confederations, acceptance of a football for use is conditional upon the football bearing one of the following three designations:

— the official "FIFA APPROVED" logo, or

— the official "FIFA INSPECTED" logo, or

— the reference "INTERNATIONAL MATCHBALL STANDARD"

Such a designation on a football indicates that it has been tested officially and found to be in compliance with specific technical requirements, different for each category and additional to the minimum specifications stipulated in Law 2. The list of the additional requirements specific to each of the respective categories must be approved by the International F.A. Board. The institutes conducting the tests are subject to the approval of FIFA.

Member association competitions may require the use of balls bearing any one of these three designations.

In all other matches, the ball used must satisfy the requirements of Law 2.

Decision 2

In FIFA competition matches and in competition matches organised under the auspices of the confederations and member associations, no kind of commercial advertising on the ball is permitted, except for the emblem of the competition, the competition organiser and the authorised trademark of the manufacturer. The competition regulations may restrict the size and number of such markings.

Law 3 – The Number of Players

Players

A match is played by two teams, each consisting of not more than eleven players, one of whom is the goalkeeper. A match may not start if either team consists of fewer than seven players.

Official Competitions

Up to a maximum of three substitutes may be used in any match played in an official competition organised under the auspices of FIFA, the confederations or the member associations.

The rules of the competition must state how many substitutes may be nominated, from three up to a maximum of seven.

Other Matches

In national A team matches, up to a maximum of six substitutes may be used.

In all other matches, a greater number of substitutes may be used provided that:

- the teams concerned reach agreement on a maximum number;
- the referee is informed before the match.

If the referee is not informed, or if no agreement is reached before the match, no more than six substitutes are allowed.

All Matches

— In all matches, the names of the substitutes must be given to the referee prior to the start of the match. Substitutes not so named may not take part in the match.

Substitution Procedure

To replace a player by a substitute, the following conditions must be observed:

— the referee is informed before any proposed substitution is made;

— a substitute only enters the field of play after the player being replaced has left and after receiving a signal from the referee;

— a substitute only enters the field of play at the halfway line and during a stoppage in the match;

— a substitution is completed when a substitute enters the field of play;

— from that moment, the substitute becomes a player and the player he has replaced ceases to be a player;

— a player who has been replaced takes no further part in the match;

— all substitutes are subject to the authority and jurisdiction of the referee, whether called upon to play or not

Changing the Goalkeeper

Any of the other players may change places with the goalkeeper, provided that:

— the referee is informed before the change is made;

— the change is made during a stoppage in the match.

Infringements/Sanctions

If a substitute enters the field of play without the referee's permission:

— play is stopped;

— the substitute is cautioned, shown the yellow card and required to leave the field of play;

— play is restarted with an indirect free kick at the place the ball was located when play was stopped

If a player changes places with the goalkeeper without the referee's permission before the change is made:

— play continues;

— the players concerned are cautioned and shown the yellow card when the ball is next out of play.

For any other infringements of this Law:

— the players concerned are cautioned and shown the yellow card.

Restart of Play

If play is stopped by the referee to administer a caution:

— the match is restarted by an indirect free kick, to be taken by a player of the opposing team from the place where the ball was located when play was stopped.

Players and Substitutes Sent Off

— A player who has been sent off before the kick-off may be replaced only by one of the named substitutes.

— A named substitute who has been sent off, either before the kick-off or after play has started, may not be replaced.

Decisions of the International F.A. Board

— *Decision 1*: Subject to the overriding conditions of Law 3, the minimum number of players in a team is left to the discretion of member associations. The Board is of the opinion, however, that a match should not continue if there are fewer than seven players in either team.

— *Decision 2*: A team official may convey tactical instructions to the players during the match and he must return to his position after giving these instructions. All officials must remain within the confines of the technical area, where such an area is provided, and they must behave in a responsible manner.

LAW 4 – THE PLAYERS' EQUIPMENT

Safety

A player must not use equipment or wear anything that is dangerous to himself or another player (including any kind of jewellery).

Jewellery

— All items of jewellery are potentially dangerous. The term "dangerous" can sometimes be ambiguous and controversial, therefore in order to be uniform and consistent any kind of jewellery has to be forbidden.

— Players are not allowed to use tape to cover jewellery. Taping jewellery is not adequate protection.

— Rings, earrings, leather or rubber bands are not necessary to play and the only thing they can bring about is injury.

In order to avoid "last minute" problems, teams should inform their players in advance.

Basic Equipment

The basic compulsory equipment of a player comprises the following separate items:

— jersey or shirt;

— shorts – if thermal undershorts are worn, they are of the same main colour as the shorts;

— stockings;

— shinguards;

— footwear.

Shinguards

— are covered entirely by the stockings;

— are made of a suitable material (rubber, plastic, or similar substances);

— provide a reasonable degree of protection.

Goalkeepers

— each goalkeeper wears colours that distinguish him from the other players, the referee and the assistant referees.

Non-Basic Equipment

— A player must not use equipment or wear anything that is dangerous to himself/herself or another player

— Modern protective equipment such as headgear, facemasks, knee and arm protectors made of soft, lightweight, padded material are not considered to be dangerous and are therefore permitted

— New technology has made sports spectacles much safer, both for the players themselves and for other players

Infringements/Sanctions

For any infringement of this Law:

— play need not be stopped;

— the player at fault is instructed by the referee to leave the field of play to correct his equipment;

— the player leaves the field of play when the ball next ceases to be in play, unless he has already corrected his equipment;

— any player required to leave the field of play to correct his equipment does not re-enter without the referee's permission;

— the referee checks that the player's equipment is correct before allowing him to re-enter the field of play;

— the player is only allowed to re-enter the field of play when the ball is out of play.

A player who has been required to leave the field of play because of an infringement of this Law and who enters (or re-enters) the field of play without the referee's permission is cautioned and shown the yellow card.

Restart of Play

If play is stopped by the referee to administer a caution:

— the match is restarted by an indirect free kick taken by a player of the opposing side, from the place where the ball was located when the referee stopped the match.

Decisions of the International F.A. Board

Decision 1

— Players must not reveal undershirts that contain slogans or advertising.

— A player removing his jersey to reveal slogans or advertising will be sanctioned by the competition organiser.

— Jerseys must have sleeves.

Law 5 – The Referee

The Authority of The Referee

— Each match is controlled by a referee who has full authority to enforce the Laws of the Game in connection with the match to which he has been appointed.

Powers and Duties

The Referee:

— enforces the Laws of the Game;

— controls the match in co-operation with the assistant referees and, where applicable, with the fourth official;

— ensures that any ball used meets the requirements of Law 2;

— ensures that the players' equipment meets the requirements of Law 4;

— acts as timekeeper and keeps a record of the match;

— stops, suspends or terminates the match, at his discretion, for any infringements of the Laws;

— stops, suspends or terminates the match because of outside interference of any kind;

— stops the match if, in his opinion, a player is seriously injured and ensures that he is removed from the field of play. An injured player may only return to the field of play after the match has restarted;

— allows play to continue until the ball is out of play if a player is, in his opinion, only slightly injured;

Powers and Duties

— ensures that any player bleeding from a wound leaves the field of play. The player may only return on receiving a signal from the referee, who must be satisfied that the bleeding has stopped;

— allows play to continue when the team against which an offence has been committed will benefit from such an advantage and penalises the original offence if the anticipated advantage does not ensue at that time;

— punishes the more serious offence when a player commits more than one offence at the same time;

— takes disciplinary action against players guilty of cautionable and sending-off offences. He is not obliged to take this action immediately but must do so when the ball next goes out of play;

— takes action against team officials who fail to conduct themselves in a responsible manner and may, at his discretion, expel them from the field of play and its immediate surrounds;

— acts on the advice of assistant referees regarding incidents that he has not seen;

— ensures that no unauthorised persons enter the field of play;

— restarts the match after it has been stopped;

— provides the appropriate authorities with a match report, which includes information on any disciplinary action taken against players, and/or team officials and any other incidents that occurred before, during or after the match.

Decisions of The Referee

— The decisions of the referee regarding facts connected with play are final.

— The referee may only change a decision on realising that it is incorrect or, at his discretion, on the advice of an assistant referee, provided that he has not restarted play or terminated the match.

Decisions of the International F.A. Board

Decision 1

A referee (or where applicable, an assistant referee or fourth official) is not held liable for: any kind of injury suffered by a player, official or spectator; any damage to property of any kind; any other loss suffered by any individual, club, company, association or other body, which is due or which may be due to any decision that he may take under the terms of the Laws of the Game or in respect of the normal procedures required to hold, play and control a match.

This may include:

— a decision that the condition of the field of play or its surrounds or that the weather conditions are such as to allow or not to allow a match to take place;

— a decision to abandon a match for whatever reason;

— a decision as to the condition of the fixtures or equipment used during a match including the goalposts, crossbar, flagposts and the ball;

— a decision to stop or not to stop a match due to spectator interference or any problem in the spectator area;

— a decision to stop or not to stop play to allow an injured player to be removed from the field of play for treatment;

— a decision to request or insist that an injured player be removed from the field of play for treatment;

— a decision to allow or not to allow a player to wear certain apparel or equipment;

— a decision (in so far as this may be his responsibility) to allow or not to allow any persons (including team or stadium officials, security officers, photographers or other media representatives) to be present in the vicinity of the field of play;

— any other decision that he may take in accordance with the Laws of the Game or in conformity with his duties under the terms of FIFA, confederation, member association or league rules or regulations under which the match is played.

Decision 2

In tournaments or competitions where a fourth official is appointed, his role and duties must be in accordance with the guidelines approved by the International F.A. Board.

Decision 3

Facts connected with play shall include whether a goal is scored or not and the result of the match.

LAW 6 – THE ASSISTANT REFEREES

Duties

Two assistant referees are appointed whose duties, subject to the decision of the referee, are to indicate:

— when the whole of the ball has passed out of the field of play;

— which side is entitled to a corner kick, goal kick or throw-in;

— when a player may be penalised for being in an offside position;

— when a substitution is requested;

— when misconduct or any other incident has occurred out of the view of the referee;

— when offences have been committed whenever the assistants are closer to the action than the referee (this includes, in particular circumstances, offences committed in the penalty area);

— whether, at penalty kicks, the goalkeeper has moved forward before the ball has been kicked and if the ball has crossed the line.

Assistance

— The assistant referees also assist the referee to control the match in accordance with the Laws of the Game. In particular, they may enter the field of play to help control the 9.15m distance.

— In the event of undue interference or improper conduct, the referee will relieve an assistant referee of his duties and make a report to the appropriate authorities.

LAW 7 THE DURATION OF THE MATCH

Periods of Play

— The match lasts two equal periods of 45 minutes, unless otherwise mutually agreed between the referee and the two participating teams.

— Any agreement to alter the periods of play (for example to reduce each half to 40 minutes because of insufficient light) must be made before the start of play and must comply with competition rules.

Half-Time Interval

— Players are entitled to an interval at half-time.

— The half-time interval must not exceed 15 minutes.

— Competition rules must state the duration of the half-time interval.

— The duration of the half-time interval may be altered only with the consent of the referee.

Allowance for Time Lost

Allowance is made in either period for all time lost through:

— substitution(s);

— assessment of injury to players;

Allowance for Time Lost

— removal of injured players from the field of play for treatment;

— wasting time;

— any other cause.

— The allowance for time lost is at the discretion of the referee.

Penalty Kick

— If a penalty kick has to be taken or retaken, the duration of either half is extended until the penalty kick is completed.

Abandoned Match

— An abandoned match is replayed unless the competition rules provide otherwise.

Law 8 – The Start and Restart of Play

Preliminaries

— A coin is tossed and the team that wins the toss decides which goal it will attack in the first half of the match.

— The other team takes the kick-off to start the match.
— The team that wins the toss takes the kick-off to start the second half of the match.
— In the second half of the match, the teams change ends and attack the opposite goals.

Kick-off

A kick-off is a way of starting or restarting play:

— at the start of the match;
— after a goal has been scored;
— at the start of the second half of the match;
— at the start of each period of extra time, where applicable.

A goal may be scored directly from the kick-off.

Procedure

— all players are in their own half of the field.
— the opponents of the team taking the kick-off are at least 9.15 m (10 yds) from the ball until it is in play.
— the ball is stationary on the centre mark.
— the referee gives a signal.
— the ball is in play when it is kicked and moves forward.
— the kicker does not touch the ball a second time until it has touched another player.

After a team scores a goal, the kick-off is taken by the other team.

Infringements/Sanctions

If the kicker touches the ball a second time before it has touched another player:

— an indirect free kick is awarded to the opposing team to be taken from the place where the infringement occurred.

For any other infringement of the kick-off procedure:

— the kick-off is retaken.

Dropped Ball

— A dropped ball is a way of restarting the match after a temporary stoppage that becomes necessary, while the ball is in play, for any reason not mentioned elsewhere in the Laws of the Game.

Procedure

— The referee drops the ball at the place where it was located when play was stopped.

— Play restarts when the ball touches the ground.

Infringements/Sanctions

The ball is dropped again:

— if it is touched by a player before it makes contact with the ground;

— if the ball leaves the field of play after it makes contact with the ground, without a player touching it.

Special Circumstances

— A free kick awarded to the defending team inside its own goal area is taken from any point within the goal area.

— An indirect free kick awarded to the attacking team in its opponents' goal area is taken from the goal area line parallel to the goal line at the point nearest to where the infringement occurred.

— A dropped ball to restart the match after play has been temporarily stopped inside the goal area takes place on the goal area line parallel to the goal line at the point nearest to where the ball was located when play was stopped.

LAW 9 – THE BALL IN AND OUT OF PLAY

Ball Out of Play

The ball is out of play when:

— it has wholly crossed the goal line or touch line, whether on the ground or in the air

— play has been stopped by the referee.

Ball In Play

The ball is in play at all other times, including when:

— it rebounds from a goalpost, crossbar or corner flagpost and remains in the field of play;

— it rebounds from either the referee or an assistant referee when they are on the field of play.

LAW 10 – THE METHOD OF SCORING

Goal Scored

A goal is scored when the whole of the ball passes over the goal line, between the goalposts and under the crossbar, provided that no infringement of the Laws of the Game has been committed previously by the team scoring the goal.

Winning Team

The team scoring the greater number of goals during a match is the winner. If both teams score an equal number of goals, or if no goals are scored, the match is drawn.

Competition Rules

When competition rules require there to be a winning team after a match or home-and-away tie, only the following procedures, which have been approved by the International F.A. Board, are permitted

— Away goals rule;

— Extra time;

— Kicks from the penalty mark.

LAW 11 – OFFSIDE

Offside Position

It is not an offence in itself to be in an offside position. A player is in an offside position if:

— he is nearer to his opponents' goal line than both the ball and the second last opponent.

A player is not in an offside position if:

— he is in his own half of the field of play or

— he is level with the second last opponent or

— he is level with the last two opponents.

Offence

A player in an offside position is only penalised if, at the moment the ball touches or is played by one of his team, he is, in the opinion of the referee, involved in active play by:

— interfering with play or

— interfering with an opponent or

— gaining an advantage by being in that position.

No Offence

There is no offside offence if a player receives the ball directly from:

— a goal kick or
— a throw-in or
— a corner kick

Infringements/Sanctions

— For any offside offence, the referee awards an indirect free kick to the opposing team to be taken from the place where the infringement occurred.

Law 12 – Fouls and Misconduct

Fouls and misconduct are penalised as follows:

Direct Free Kick

A direct free kick is awarded to the opposing team if a player commits any of the following six offences in a manner considered by the referee to be careless, reckless or using excessive force:

— kicks or attempts to kick an opponent
— trips or attempts to trip an opponent
— jumps at an opponent
— charges an opponent
— strikes or attempts to strike an opponent
— pushes an opponent

A direct free kick is also awarded to the opposing team if a player commits any of the following four offences:

— tackles an opponent to gain possession of the ball, making contact with the opponent before touching the ball
— holds an opponent
— spits at an opponent
— handles the ball deliberately (except for the goalkeeper within his own penalty area).

A direct free kick is taken from where the offence occurred.

Fouls and misconduct are penalised as follows:

Penalty Kick

— A penalty kick is awarded if any of the above ten offences is committed by a player inside his own penalty area, irrespective of the position of the ball, provided it is in play.

Indirect Free Kick

An indirect free kick is awarded to the opposing team if a goalkeeper, inside his own penalty area, commits any of the following four offences:

— takes more than six seconds while controlling the ball with his hands before releasing it from his possession

— touches the ball again with his hands after it has been released from his possession and has not touched any other player

— touches the ball with his hands after it has been deliberately kicked to him by a team-mate

— touches the ball with his hands after he has received it directly from a throw-in taken by a team-mate.

An indirect free kick is also awarded to the opposing team if a player, in the opinion of the referee:

— plays in a dangerous manner

— impedes the progress of an opponent

Fouls and misconduct are penalised as follows:

Indirect Free Kick

— prevents the goalkeeper from releasing the ball from his hands;

— commits any other offence, not previously mentioned in Law 12, for which play is stopped to caution or dismiss a player.

The indirect free kick is taken from where the offence occurred.

Disciplinary Sanctions

Only a player or substitute or substituted player may be shown the red or yellow card.

The referee has the authority to take disciplinary sanctions, as from the moment he enters the field of play until he leaves the field of play after the final whistle.

Cautionable Offences

A player is cautioned and shown the yellow card if he commits any of the following seven offences:

1. is guilty of unsporting behaviour
2. shows dissent by word or action
3. persistently infringes the Laws of the Game
4. delays the restart of play

Cautionable Offences

5. fails to respect the required distance when play is restarted with a corner kick, free kick or throw-in
6. enters or re-enters the field of play without the referee's permission
7. deliberately leaves the field of play without the referee's permission.

A substitute or substituted player is cautioned and shown the yellow card if he commits any of the following three offences:

1. is guilty of unsporting behaviour

2. shows dissent by word or action
3. delays the restart of play

Sending-Off Offences

A player, substitute or substituted player is sent off and shown the red card if he commits any of the following seven offences:

1. is guilty of serious foul play
2. is guilty of violent conduct
3. spits at an opponent or any other person
4. denies the opposing team a goal or an obvious goalscoring opportunity by deliberately handling the ball (this does not apply to a goalkeeper within his own penalty area)
5. denies an obvious goalscoring opportunity to an opponent moving towards the player's goal by an offence punishable by a free kick or a penalty kick
6. uses offensive or insulting or abusive language and/ or gestures
7. receives a second caution in the same match.

A player, substitute or substituted player who has been sent off and shown the red card must leave the vicinity of the field of play and the technical area.

Decisions of the International F.A. Board

Decision 1

A player who commits a cautionable or sending-off offence, either on or off the field of play, whether directed towards an opponent, a team-mate, the referee, an assistant referee or any other person, is disciplined according to the nature of the offence committed.

Decision 2

The goalkeeper is considered to be in control of the ball by touching it with any part of his hand or arms. Possession of the ball includes the goalkeeper deliberately parrying the ball, but does not include the circumstances where, in the opinion of the referee, the ball rebounds accidentally from the goalkeeper, for example after he has made a save.

Decision 3

Subject to the terms of Law 12 , a player may pass the ball to his own goalkeeper using his head or chest or knee, etc. If, however, in the opinion of the referee, a player uses a deliberate trick while the ball is in play in order to circumvent the Law, the player is guilty of unsporting behaviour. He is cautioned, shown the yellow card and an indirect free kick is awarded to the opposing team from the place where the infringement occurred.

A player using a deliberate trick to circumvent the Law while he is taking a free kick is cautioned for unsporting behaviour and shown the yellow card. The free kick is retaken. In such circumstances, it is irrelevant whether the goalkeeper subsequently touches the ball with his hands or not. The offence is committed by the player in attempting to circumvent both the letter and the spirit of Law 12 .

Decision 4

A tackle, which endangers the safety of an opponent, must be sanctioned as serious foul play.

Decision 5

Any simulating action anywhere on the field, which is intended to deceive the referee, must be sanctioned as unsporting behaviour.

Decision 6

Removing a jersey:

— A player who removes his jersey when celebrating a goal must be cautioned for unsporting behaviour.

— Removing a jersey after a goal has been scored is unnecessary and players must avoid such excessive displays of celebration.

— Removing a jersey is defined as removing the jersey over the head or covering the head with the jersey.

LAW 13 – FREE KICKS

Types of Free Kicks

Free kicks are either direct or indirect.

For both direct and indirect free kicks, the ball must be stationary when the kick is taken and the kicker does not touch the ball a second time until it has touched another player.

The Direct Free Kick

— If a direct free kick is kicked directly into the opponents' goal, a goal is awarded.

— If a direct free kick is kicked directly into the team's own goal, a corner kick is awarded to the opposing team.

The Indirect Free Kick

Signal

The referee indicates an indirect free kick by raising his arm above his head. He maintains his arm in that position until the kick has been taken and the ball has touched another player or goes out of play.

Ball Enters the Goal

A goal can be scored only if the ball subsequently touches another player before it enters the goal.

— if an indirect free kick is kicked directly into the opponents' goal, a goal kick is awarded.

— if an indirect free kick is kicked directly into the team's own goal, a corner kick is awarded to the opposing team.

Position of Free Kick

Free Kick Inside the Penalty Area

Direct or indirect free kick to the defending team:

— all opponents are at least 9.15 m (10 yds) from the ball.

— all opponents remain outside the penalty area until the ball is in play.

— the ball is in play when it is kicked directly beyond the penalty area.

— a free kick awarded in the goal area is taken from any point inside that area.

Indirect free kick to the attacking team:

— all opponents are at least 9.15 m (10 yds) from the ball until it is in play, unless they are on their own goal line between the goalposts.

— the ball is in play when it is kicked and moves.

— an indirect free kick awarded inside the goal area is taken from that part of the goal area line which runs parallel to the goal line, at the point nearest to where the infringement occurred.

Free Kick Outside the Penalty Area

— all opponents are at least 9.15 m (10 yds) from the ball until it is in play.

— the ball is in play when it is kicked and moves.

— the free kick is taken from the place where the infringement occurred.

Infringements/Sanctions

If, when a free kick is taken, an opponent is closer to the ball than the required distance:

— the kick is retaken.

If, when a free kick is taken by the defending team from inside its own penalty area, the ball is not kicked directly into play:

— the kick is retaken.

Free kick taken by a player other than the goalkeeper

If, after the ball is in play, the kicker touches the ball a second time (except with his hands) before it has touched another player:

— an indirect free kick is awarded to the opposing team, the kick to be taken from the place where the infringement occurred

If, after the ball is in play, the kicker deliberately handles the ball before it has touched another player:

— a direct free kick is awarded to the opposing team, the kick to be taken from the place where the infringement occurred

— a penalty kick is awarded if the infringement occurred inside the kicker's penalty area.

Free kick taken by the goalkeeper

If, after the ball is in play, the goalkeeper touches the ball a second time (except with his hands), before it has touched another player:

— an indirect free kick is awarded to the opposing team, the kick to be taken from the place where the infringement occurred.

If, after the ball is in play, the goalkeeper deliberately handles the ball before it has touched another player:

— a direct free kick is awarded to the opposing team if the infringement occurred outside the goalkeeper's penalty area, the kick to be taken from the place where the infringement occurred

— an indirect free kick is awarded to the opposing team if the infringement occurred inside the goalkeeper's penalty area, the kick to be taken from the place where the infringement occurred.

Law 14 – The Penalty Kick

The Penalty Kick

A penalty kick is awarded against a team that commits one of the ten offences for which a direct free kick is awarded, inside its own penalty area and while the ball is in play.

A goal may be scored directly from a penalty kick.

Additional time is allowed for a penalty kick to be taken at the end of each half or at the end of periods of extra time.

Position of the Ball and the Players

The ball:

— is placed on the penalty mark.

The player taking the penalty kick:

— is properly identified.

The defending goalkeeper:

— remains on his goal line, facing the kicker, between the goalposts until the ball has been kicked.

Position of the Ball and the Players

The players other than the kicker are located:

— inside the field of play;
— outside the penalty area;
— behind the penalty mark;
— at least 9.15 m (10 yds) from the penalty mark.

The Referee

— does not signal for a penalty kick to be taken until the players have taken up position in accordance with the Law;
— decides when a penalty kick has been completed.

Procedure

— The player taking the penalty kicks the ball forward.
— He does not play the ball a second time until it has touched another player.
— The ball is in play when it is kicked and moves forward.

When a penalty kick is taken during the normal course of play, or time has been extended at half-time or full time to allow a penalty kick to be taken or retaken, a goal is awarded if, before passing between the goalposts and under the crossbar:

— the ball touches either or both of the goalposts and/ or the crossbar, and/or the goalkeeper.

Infringements/Sanctions If the referee gives the signal for a penalty kick to be taken and, before the ball is in play, one of the following situations occurs:

The player taking the penalty kick infringes the Laws of the Game:

— the referee allows the kick to proceed.
— if the ball enters the goal, the kick is retaken.
— if the ball does not enter the goal, the referee stops

play and restarts the match with an indirect free kick to the defending team, from the place where the infringement occurred.

The goalkeeper infringes the Laws of the Game:

— the referee allows the kick to proceed.

— if the ball enters the goal, a goal is awarded.

— if the ball does not enter the goal, the kick is retaken.

A team-mate of the player taking the kick infringes the Laws of the Game:

— the referee allows the kick to proceed.

— If the ball enters the goal, the kick is retaken.

— If the ball does not enter the goal, the referee stops play and restarts the match with an indirect free kick to the defending team, from the place where the infringement occurred.

A team-mate of the goalkeeper infringes the laws of the game:

— the referee allows the kick to proceed.

— if the ball enters the goal, a goal is awarded.

— if the ball does not enter the goal, the kick is retaken.

A player of both the defending team and the attacking team infringe the Laws of the Game:

— the kick is retaken.

If, after the penalty kick has been taken: The kicker touches the ball a second time (except with his hands) before it has touched another player:

— an indirect free kick is awarded to the opposing team, the kick to be taken from the place where the infringement occurred.

The kicker deliberately handles the ball before it has touched another player:

— a direct free kick is awarded to the opposing team, the kick to be taken from the place where the infringement occurred.

The ball is touched by an outside agent as it moves forward:

— the kick is retaken.

The ball rebounds into the field of play from the goalkeeper, the crossbar or the goalposts, and is then touched by an outside agent:

— the referee stops play;

— play is restarted with a dropped ball at the place where it touched the outside agent

It is an infringement to enter the penalty area before the kick has been taken.

The goalkeeper also infringes the Laws if he moves from his goal line before the ball has been kicked.

Referees must ensure that when players infringe this Law, appropriate action is taken.

The Technical Area

Only one person at a time is authorised to convey tactical instructions and he must return to his position after giving these instructions.

Liquid Refreshments

Players are entitled to take liquid refreshments during a stoppage in the match but only on the touch line. It is not permitted to throw plastic water bags or any water containers onto the field.

LAW 15 – THE THROW-IN

A throw-in is a method of restarting play.

A goal cannot be scored directly from a throw-in.

A throw-in is awarded:

— when the whole of the ball passes over the touch line, either on the ground or in the air;

— from the point where it crossed the touch line;

— to the opponents of the player who last touched the ball.

Procedure

At the moment of delivering the ball, the thrower:

— faces the field of play;

— has part of each foot either on the touch line or on the ground outside the touch line

— uses both hands

— delivers the ball from behind and over his head

The thrower may not touch the ball again until it has touched another player.

All opponents must stand no less than 2 meters from the point at which the throw-in is taken.

The ball is in play immediately after it enters the field of play.

Infringements/Sanctions

Throw-in taken by a player other than the goalkeeper:

— If, after the ball is in play, the thrower touches the ball a second time (except with his hands) before it has touched another player:

— an indirect free kick is awarded to the opposing team, the kick to be taken from the place where the infringement occurred

If, after the ball is in play, the thrower deliberately handles the ball before it has touched another player:

— a direct free kick is awarded to the opposing team, the kick to be taken from the place where the infringement occurred

— a penalty kick is awarded if the infringement occurred inside the thrower's penalty area.

Throw-in taken by the goalkeeper:

If, after the ball is in play, the goalkeeper touches the ball a second time (except with his hands), before it has touched another player:

— an indirect free kick is awarded to the opposing team, the kick to be taken from the place where the infringement occurred

If, after the ball is in play, the goalkeeper deliberately handles the ball before it has touched another player:

— a direct free kick is awarded to the opposing team if the infringement occurred outside the goalkeeper's penalty area, the kick to be taken from the place where the infringement occurred

— an indirect free kick is awarded to the opposing team if the infringement occurred inside the goalkeeper's penalty area, the kick to be taken from the place where the infringement occurred

If an opponent unfairly distracts or impedes the thrower:

— he is cautioned for unsporting behaviour and shown the yellow card.

For any other infringement of this Law:

— the throw-in is taken by a player of the opposing team.

Law 16 – The Goal Kick

A goal kick is a method of restarting play. A goal may be scored directly from a goal kick, but only against the opposing team.

A goal kick is awarded when:

— the whole of the ball, having last touched a player of the attacking team, passes over the goal line, either on the ground or in the air, and a goal is not scored in accordance with Law 10 .

Procedure

— The ball is kicked from any point within the goal area by a player of the defending team.

— Opponents remain outside the penalty area until the ball is in play.

— The kicker does not play the ball a second time until it has touched another player.

— The ball is in play when it is kicked directly beyond the penalty area.

Infringements/Sanctions

If the ball is not kicked directly into play beyond the penalty area:

— the kick is retaken.

Goal kick taken by a player other than the goalkeeper:

If, after the ball is in play, the kicker touches the ball a second time (except with his hands) before it has touched another player:

— an indirect free kick is awarded to the opposing team, the kick to be taken from the place where the infringement occurred

If, after the ball is in play, the kicker deliberately handles the ball before it has touched another player:

— a direct free kick is awarded to the opposing team, the kick to be taken from the place where the infringement occurred

— a penalty kick is awarded if the infringement occurred inside the kicker's penalty area.

Goal kick taken by the goalkeeper:

If, after the ball is in play, the goalkeeper touches the ball a second time (except with his hands) before it has touched another player. An indirect free kick is awarded to the opposing team, the kick to be taken from the place where the infringement occurred If, after the ball is in play, the goalkeeper deliberately handles the ball before it has touched another player:

— a direct free kick is awarded to the opposing team if the infringement occurred outside the goalkeeper's penalty area, the kick to be taken from the place where the infringement occurred

— an indirect free kick is awarded to the opposing team if the infringement occurred inside the goalkeeper's penalty area, the kick to be taken from the place where the infringement occurred

For any other infringement of this Law:

— the kick is retaken.

LAW 17 – THE CORNER KICK

A corner kick is a method of restarting play. A goal may be scored directly from a corner kick, but only against the opposing team. A corner kick is awarded when:

— the whole of the ball, having last touched a player of the defending team, passes over the goal line, either on the ground or in the air, and a goal is not scored in accordance with Law 10

Procedure

The ball is placed inside the corner arc at the nearest corner flagpost.

— The corner flagpost is not moved.

— Opponents remain at least 9.15 m (10 yds) from the corner arc until the ball is in play.

— The ball is kicked by a player of the attacking team.

— The ball is in play when it is kicked and moves.

— The kicker does not play the ball a second time until it has touched another player.

If, after the ball is in play, the kicker deliberately handles the ball before it has touched another player:

— a direct free kick is awarded to the opposing team, the kick to be taken from the place where the infringement occurred

— a penalty kick is awarded if the infringement occurred inside the kicker's penalty area.

Corner kick taken by the goalkeeper:

If, after the ball is in play, the goalkeeper touches the ball a second time (except with his hands) before it has touched another player:

— an indirect free kick is awarded to the opposing team, the kick to be taken from the place where the infringement occurred

If, after the ball is in play, the goalkeeper deliberately handles the ball before it has touched another player:

— a direct free kick is awarded to the opposing team if the infringement occurred outside the goalkeeper's penalty area, the kick to be taken from the place where the infringement occurred

— an indirect free kick is awarded to the opposing team if the infringement occurred inside the goalkeeper's penalty area, the kick to be taken from the place where the infringement occurred

For any other infringement:

— the kick is retaken.

4

Formations

Formation in football describes how the players in a team are positioned on the pitch. Different formations can be used depending on whether a team wishes to play more attacking or defensive football.

Formations are described as the number of players in each area from the defensive line (not including the goalkeeper). For example 4-4-2 describes the formation as having: 4 defenders, 4 midfielders and 2 forwards. Conventionally the formation can be described with 3 numbers, although 4-numbered (e.g. 4-4-1-1) and 5-numbered formations (e.g. 4-1-2-1-2) can be used. The numbering system was not present until the 4-2-4 system was developed in the 1950s.

Formations can be altered during a game, but requires adaptations of the players to fit in to the new system. This can be due to a team wishing to defend or attack more, or even due to the loss of a player. Some formations also lend themselves to dynamically changing as players move up and down the field, e.g., the Brazilian 4-2-4 could effectively become a 2-4-4 during a match. In this way formations can be deceptive in analysing a particular team's style of play, i.e. one team could play 4-4-2 and work defensively, whereas their opposition using the same formation could play much more attacking football.

Formations are used in both professional and amateur football matches. However in amateur matches these tactics are sometimes adhered to less strictly such is the lesser severity of the occasion. Skill and discipline on behalf of the players is also needed to effectively carry out a given formation in professional football. Formations need to be chosen with the players available in mind, and some of the formations below were created to address deficits in different types of players.

According to the leading Norwegian football manager Egil Olsen, there is a large number of tactical choices that are more important than the choice of formation.

Early Days

Formations, or systems of play, have not always been with football. In 1863, when the London FA was set up, football players dribbled with the ball on their own. Only backward or lateral passes were allowed. As they were thought to slow the game down, they were rarely, if ever, used. In 1866, the rules changed. Forward passing was now allowed. But the English, the originators of the game, stuck to heads-down dribbling. Games were played with only one fullback and the other eight up in attack.

It was the Scottish that came up with the idea of passing the ball. In 1872, in the first international match, between Scotland and England, the Scots surprised the English. Why? It was due to two reasons. Firstly, the Scottish team, instead of running with the ball, was using short passes along the ground to advance the ball. Secondly, the Scottish team played using two fullbacks instead of one, cutting the number of attackers down to seven. Despite the extravagance in attack, the final score was 0-0. However, this left the English determined to come up with their own systems.

Blackburn Olympic, a club side from the north of England, won the FA Cup in 1883 with their secret weapon: wing-to-wing long passing. Their opponents, Old Etonians, from the south of England, were surprised at the use of this new technique.

The change in style of play meant that players had to be fitter, had to run around a lot more, than in the past. Also, this meant that a counterattack could develop quickly, so that the offense and defense had to be leveled out. This was done, naturally, by cutting down the number of forwards, and dropping back players into midfield.

2-3-5 (The Pyramid)

In 1884, Blackburn Rovers (England) introduced what would become the first long-term successful formation - the 2-3-5; this was originally known as the Pyramid with the numerical formation being referenced retrospectively. By the 1890s it was the standard formation in Britain and had spread all over the world. With some variations it was used by most top level teams up to the 1940s.

For the first time a balance between attacking and defending was reached. When defending, the two defenders (fullbacks) would watch out for the opponent's insides (the second and fourth players in the attacking line); while the midfielders (halfbacks) would watch for the other three forwards.

The center halfback had a key role in both helping to organize the team's attack and marking the opponent's center forward, supposedly one of their most dangerous players. This formation, also known as the Pyramid, or the classic formation, as it was used for 50 years after its invention, has only two defenders. Three midfielders and five forwards should be sufficient evidence to show that this is an attack-oriented formation. Attacking plays generally began from the center-half, who had usually two options: to pass to one of the five forwards or to dribble forward himself. The defence is manned solely by the defenders and thewing-halves, the two outside midfielders, helped out by marking the opposing wingers. The Danubian style, based loosely on the 2-3-5 and used successfully by the Austrian, Hungarian and Czechoslovakian national teams in the 1930s, was only different in one aspect. The passes used by the players were strictly kept on the ground, and no aerial passes were used.

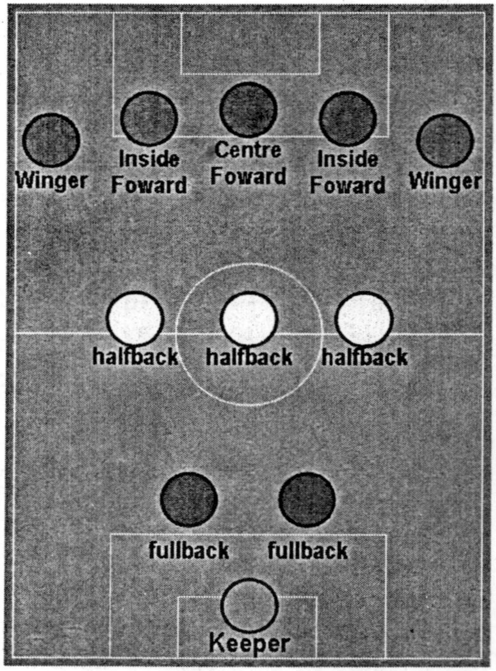

Figure 1. The 2-3-5 Formation

This formation requires defenders that have good stamina, good sense of positioning, and good tackling skills, as they have to do the defending of the goal alone. The wing-halves should be able to run fast and pass well, and possess some amount of trickery, for they will have to outwit the opposition wingers.The centre-half should have a great control of the ball, superb sense of positioning and good passing. Wingers have to be creative, have a decent aptitude in dribbling down the flanks, and be able to beat defenders with ease, for they are the suppliers of the goals, and must beat the opposing wing-halves to do so.

Great passing is another important asset for the winger, as he has to find the centre-forward in good positions to enable him to score. The centre-forward must be one man who is able to get the goals; people who can put the ball over the bar from two metres out need not apply. The centre-forward must also have a strong shot and good passing, so that in case he gets into trouble, he can pass it out to the wingers to try again.

The Italian Metodo

Another modification to the 2-3-5, implemented by Vittorio Pozzo, 1934 coach to the Italian World Cup team. It was meant to be the Danubian style, with which the Austrian team were destroying all opposition, but he had no playmaker — his centre-half was more of a defensive type — and thus no source of attacks. This problem he solved by pulling the two inside-forwards back into midfield to start off the attacks and to act as playmaker. His centre-half then took on a more defensive role. This meant that his attack looked somewhat like the M of the W-M formation. The centre-half has to be alert, as he is now a part-time "fullback" instead of a playmaker. He still helps out in attack, but just not as often. The two inside-forwards need to have the same qualities the 2-3-5 centre-half had, as they are now the offensive playmakers. The centre-forward has to be more skilful as he is the only one with the responsibility of scoring goals.

Figure 2. The Italian Metodo

The W-M Method

The 1925 amendment of the offside rule meant that an attacking player need only keep 2 opponents in front of him and not 3 as stated before. This made the offside trap a much more challenging proposition. If one defender made a mistake, then the goalkeeper would be left on his own to defend the goal..Unsurprisingly, the number of goals scored in the English First Division rose by 43%, from 1,192 to 1,703.

The perceptive Arsenal manager Herbert Chapman, along with his captain Charlie Buchan, devised a system to stop this problem after a 7-0 drubbing by Newcastle. They noticed that it was the centre-forward doing most of the goalscoring. Thus, the centre-half was pulled back to become the stopper, or the centre-back. To fill up the gap created in midfield, the two inside-forwards were pulled back to create a four-man midfield which the Italians called the magic square. The team thus had the general shape of a W of defensive players and an M of attack-minded players, giving rise to the name W-M. The typical W-M centre-forward was brawny and could score well.

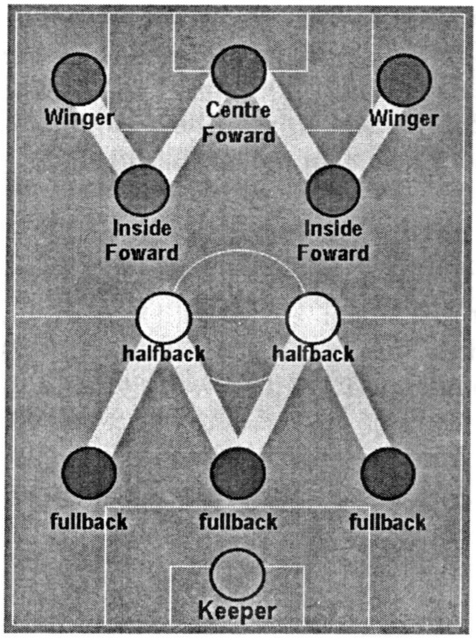

Figure 3. The W-M Method

Arsenal's W-M was very successful because of a few special touches that Chapman put in: Firstly, his defensive W was a lopsided one. This meant that when an attack began on the opposition's left flank, Arsenal's rightback would come in for the challenge, while Arsenal's defensive right midfielder, stopper, defensive left midfielder and leftback moved to respectively deeper positions as shown in the diagram to your right.

Secondly, the Arsenal wingers could also cut in to score goals. Thirdly, one of the inside-forwards was used as a playmaker, to fill up the gap from the loss of the centre-half.

Brazil's version of the W-M in 1950 was the diagonal system, with only 2 fullbacks, covering the centre and right part of the defensive third of the field, the left flank being the job of a withdrawn left midfielder who was expected to help out in attack. This led to some defensive vulnerability, but lots of attacking firepower. Its vulnerabilities were only exposed once, by the Swiss, which held the Brazilian team to a 2-2 draw with their bolt system. This was enough, and the Brazilians switched to an orthodox version of the W-M, which proved very successful, taking them to the Final where they lost to a highly adapted Uruguayan team using a sort of metodo which was really more like a 4-3-3.

Advice on the W-M: To use the orthodox W-M successfully, the defense has to be alert, and passing within the team must be good. In other words, as with all other formations, teamwork has to be strong so that communication is done efficiently. Scoring must not be a difficulty to the forwards as there are now less forwards up front, and where attacking play is concerned, the midfield has to help out as well as the movements upfront have to start with the midfield.

To use the Arsenal version, your wingers should have about the same skills as a 2-3-5 centre-forward, for scoring goals is another of the new responsibilities of the wingers. You can use all four midfielders as a bridge between the defense and offense, as the role of playmaker will be taken up by one of the inside forwards. For the Brazilian version, strong defenders with lots of stamina are the thing to have because if the withdrawn left midfielder gets caught out, then the two backs will have to cover the entire defensive third of the pitch.

THE SWISS VERROU FORMATION

Also known as the Swiss bolt formation, the verrou is a system of play that requires disciplined and highly-fit players who can afford to run hard and long throughout the entire game and can act in both offensive and defensive roles. Generally played with 3 defenders, 3 midfielders and 4 forwards, the entire team advanced on attack. Even the defence was shifted up to the centre of the field, in the neutral third of the pitch. But the special feature of the verrou was the defence.

Figure 4. The Swiss verrou

On loss of the ball, all ten outfield players retreated, and their functions were as follows: the four forwards would harass the opposing attackers, slowing the attack down and giving time for the rest of the team to move back into place. The midfield "line" shifted further back, allowing the centre-half to take the position of the centre-back. The defense retreated to just outside the penalty area, and the former centre-back now became the deep centre-back, the player behind all the rest save the goalkeeper. This feature of the verrou, the deep centre-back, will be seen later on in another system.

Highly fit, disciplined players are required, as stated above, along with good teamwork and good sense of positioning. This is not a very easy formation to use, because of the fitness and discipline required.

The Catenaccio Formation

In 1947, Nereo Rocco became the new coach of Triestina, a small club in Italy's Serie A. Triestina was then only barely surviving in the league. Rocco's catenaccio system saw Triestina shooting up to second in the league later that season. Catenaccio at its most attacking is played with a 1-3-3-3 formation. The most important part of the catenaccio was the focus on defence. Though not as outright defensive as the verrou, this defensive alignment was also important — it led to football's darkest era when sterile, goalless matches were produced.

Figure 5. Catenaccio

Three of the fullbacks had man-to-man marking duties, and the deep centre-back, the solitary "1" behind the defence, would be the libero, the free man. This libero would have no marking duties, and would patrol the backline to cover up in case a fullback made a mistake. Almost all of the game was spent with long balls probing the defence, or sending only the forward line to attack, so that there would be enough players left to defend if a counterattack from the opposition developed. At its most defensive, a catenaccio team can even play with a 1-4-3-2 or 1-4-4-1 formation.

The W-W Formation

Hungary's problem in the 1950s was the centre-forward. Along with the W-M came the brawny centre-forward, which is what the Hungarian team did not have in 1953. Gustav Sebes, the 1953 coach of the Hungarian national team, changed the W-M to a W-W in the following manner:

Figure 6. W-W method

He pulled the centre-forward back to play as a playmaker, taking over the role of the two inside-forwards. They were instead pushed up to give Hungary a two-pronged strikeforce. The wingers were pulled back to give a 5-man midfield.

Hungary's national team also attacked as a unit, with the backline moving into the opposing half. This adventurous play was open to counterattacks, via a long ball over the desperately out-of-place defence and speedy forwards. But the likelihood of this was lessened by the even more adventurous play of goalkeeper Gyula Grosics, who often came out of the 18-yard box to clear loose balls.

Advice on the W-W: If the W-W is to be used successfully, you need two centre-forwards, one playmaker, and two very good runners who can play up and down the wing. This is for the forward line. For the defensive W you need to have five alert players who can run well, have plenty of stamina and pass well.

4-2-4 Formation

The 4-2-4 formation attempts to combine strong offence with strong defence, and was conceived as a reaction to WM's stiffness. It could also be considered a further development of the WW. The 4-2-4 was the first formation to be described using numbers.

While the initial developments leading to the 4-2-4 were devised by Márton Bukovi, the credit for creating the 4-2-4 lies with two different people: Flávio Costa, the Brazilian national coach in the early 1950s, as well as another Hungarian Béla Guttman. These tactics seemed to be developed independently, with the Brazilians discussing these ideas while the Hungarians seemed to be putting them into motion. However the fully developed 4-2-4 was only 'perfected' in Brazil in the late 1950s.

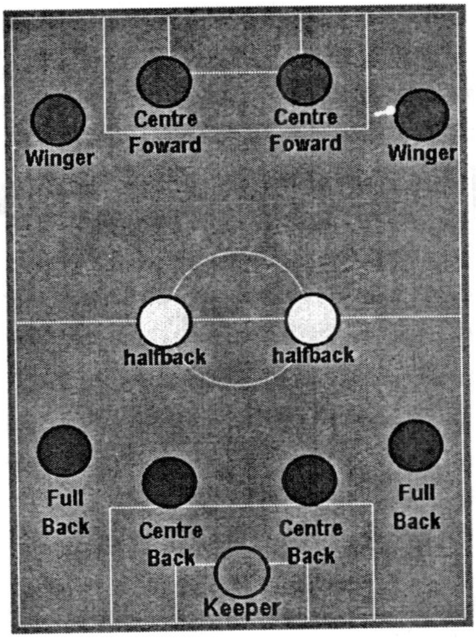

Figure 7. The 4-2-4 formation

Costa published his ideas, the "diagonal system", in the Brazilian newspaper O Cruzeiro, using schematics as the ones used here. The "diagonal system" was another precursor of the 4-2-4 and was created to spur improvisation in players. Guttman himself moved to Brazil later in the 1950s to help develop these tactical ideas using the experience of Hungarian coaches.

The 4-2-4 formation made use of the increasing players skills and fitness, aiming to effectively use 6 defenders and 6 forwards, with the midfielders performing both tasks. The 4th defender increased the number of defensive players but mostly allowed them to be closer together, thus enabling effective cooperation among them, the point being that a stronger defence would allow an even stronger attack.

The relatively empty midfield relied on defenders that should now be able not only to steal the ball, but also hold it, pass it or even run with it and start an attack. So this formation required that all players, including defenders, are somehow skillful and with initiative, making it a perfect fit for the Brazilian players mind. The 4-2-4 needed a high level of tactical awareness as having only 2 midfielders could lead to defensive problems. The system was also fluid enough to allow the formation to change throughout play.

4-2-4 was first used with success at club level in Brazil by São Paulo and Santos, and was used by Brazil in their wins at 1958 World Cup and 1970 World Cup, both featuring Pelé, and Zagallo who played in the first and coached the second. The formation was quickly adopted throughout the world after the Brazilian success. If the Brazilian style of the 4-2-4 is to be played successfully, two of the fullbacks in your starting lineup have to have good ball control, speed, good shooting and passing, and some amount of creativity, for sometimes they will have to function as wingers. Speed is one of the more important as the fullbacks will have to move back when a counterattack develops, or when they have made a mistake. The fullbacks should NOT move back the moment they have passed the ball away. When they have lost the ball, they should try to get the ball back, to proceed with the attack, rather than to mindlessly clear it upfield.

4-3-3 Formation

The focus in the 1962 World Cup in Chile was shifted to defensive tactics, and the Brazilian team mirrored this trend. Aimoré Moreira, the Brazilian coach, shifted Mario Zagalo back into midfield. In 1958, he was a winger who occasionally dropped back to help out in defensive duties in midfield. By 1962 he was shifted to midfield, thus becoming a left midfielder who sometimes helped out with attacking moves on the left wing.

Played with 4 fullbacks, 3 midfielders, and 3 attackers including a winger, the 4-3-3 is both a defensive formation and an attacking formation. The Argentinian flavour of 4-3-3, played in the 1978 World Cup, was highly attack-oriented. Four fullbacks with zonal marking was the standard then in Argentine club sides. However, so many players tended to move forward that the formation ended up looking like a 2-3-5 at times. The modified 3-man forward line consisted of 2 wingers and a centre-forward. Osvaldo Ardiles and Mario Kempes were "midfielders" on paper, but were really "inside-forwards", attacking from time to time.

To play the Brazilian flavour well, the same things as the 4-2-4 are needed: overlapping fullbacks. For the Argentinian flavour, all you really need are attacking players. Quite a few of them. They must also have above average ball control, and good sense of positioning as always.

4-4-2 Formation

This adaptable formation is the most common in football today, so well known that it has even inspired a magazine title, FourFourTwo. The midfielders are required to work hard to support both the defense and the attack: one of the central midfielders is expected to go upfield as often as possible to support the forward pair, while the other will play a "holding role", shielding the defense; the two wide midfield players must move up the flanks to the goal line in attacks and yet also protect the fullback wide defenders.

This is a tamer formation than the 4-2-4, because there are less forwards used here. The forward line has been cut down to 2 forwards, and thus no real wingers were used. Of course, play still extended out to the wings, but this was only around the midfield area. This shortening of the paragraphs reflects the amount of tactical innovations in the time period: this was one of the last new tactics to come about.

Figure 8. The 4-4-2 formation

England's midfield was interesting as it used Nobby Stiles as a sweeper in front of the defensive line. Stiles's hard and effective tackling meant that the defenders could concentrate on their man-marking duties. England's other special touch was that the strikers' off-the-ball running would draw the opposing defenders away and thus create space which the midfielders, Charlton and Ball, could put to good use.

In the 1982 World Cup, France and Brazil had their own versions of the 4-4-2. France used a sweeper while

Brazil used zonal marking and overlapping fullbacks. However, due to the lax refereeing, and their finishing problems up front, these two teams were knocked out by the end of the first round.

To use this formation well, no wingers are needed. The forwards used must be of high standard, as they are the ones shouldering the full responsibility of getting the goals. Off-the-ball running, or decoying, is a good practice. This allows for more chances as it will pull defenders away from the line of action, giving the ball-player a clear path to goal. Faking passes might go well with this.

Total Football

In football, Total Football is a system where a player who moves out of his or her position is replaced by another from his or her team, thus retaining their intended organizational structure. In this fluid system no footballer is fixed in his or her intended outfield role; anyone can be successively an attacker, a midfielder and a defender. Total Football depends largely on the adaptability of each footballer within the team to succeed. Many believe the foundations of Total Football originally stem from the Push and run style of play.

The foundations for Total Football were laid by Jack Reynolds, who was the manager of Ajax Amsterdam for 33 years in the early 20th century. Rinus Michels, who played under Reynolds, later went on to become manager of Ajax himself and refined the concept into what is known today as "Total Football" (Totaalvoetbal, in Dutch), using it in his training for the Ajax squad and the Netherlands national team in the 1970s. A pupil of Michels, Johan Cruyff, who played in both the Ajax and Dutch national teams under him later exported the system to teams such as FC Barcelona. The term Total

Football is also used to describe the effective, dominating play of West German football in the 1970s.

The ill-fated Austrian "Wunderteam" of the 1930s is also credited in some circles as being the first national team to play Total Football. It is no coincidence that Ernst Happel, a talented Austrian player in the 1940's and 50's was coach in the Netherlands in the late 1960's and early 70's. He introduced a kind of toughness at ADO and Feyenoord that was lacking before in the Dutch way of playing.

Pioneered (in the World Cup, at any rate) by the Dutch and the Germans in the 1974 World Cup in West Germany, the team plays as one giant unit. There are no fixed roles in a team (except the goalkeeper of course.) When a fullback has the ball and thinks he can start an attack, he can move up on his own, and any player, even a forward, can help out by moving back to fill up the gap in defense. In other words, the team is not divided into defenders, midfielders and forwards; anyone can do anything (intelligently, of course) he wishes to.

However, as total football is nothing but 10 skilful players having fun, the Dutch team lost its light springy image in 1978 without Johan Cruyff, star of the 1974 Dutch World Cup team, who announced he would not play in that World Cup. Franz Beckenbauer played in the libero position for Germany, and often moved up to join in the attacks, thus bewildering the opposition fullbacks who already had their own man-marking assignments. The German flavour was also diluted when Franz Beckenbauer followed Cruyff and "retired" for the '78 World Cup.

This style of play is not really a formation. Rather, the advantages of using this against an opponent is that the opposition will spend their time trying to figure out what tactics your team is using while your team can take advantage of the confusion and score. This should only be used, however, if the communication and rapport between the players is very good, and that most players have above average ball skills. Otherwise passes might go off target, possession might be lost, and big gaps might be created that the opposition can use to devastating effect. In other words, this is an all-or-nothing formation, either it works well, or it backfires badly. Not much of an in-between.

As far as new tactical developments were concerned, by 1982, the coaches and players seem to have run out of inspiration. The FIFA technical study group, composed of coaches who would analyse the play after each World Cup, reported, in 1982, 1986 and 1990 that "nothing startlingly new was produced".

The systems of play we reviewed above are just general guides to how your team should play. Tactics should always be adopted to the qualities of the team that uses it. However, this is sadly not the case. Most of the time, a team rigidly adheres to a tactic, and as a result, when a slight variation is introduced into their opponents' play, the team crumbles, making a dismal comedy of itself.

Attitude should dominate the selection of a particular tactic. For example, if you try to follow the Brazilian 4-4-2 with overlapping fullbacks and all, but your team does not have good overlapping fullbacks, the strategy will fall flat on its face so will your team. Of course, if the formation your team plays with is well-suited to your team, then your team should play better than before.

5

Basic Football Skills

This chapter consists of some basic skills needed to play good soccer. Apart from goalkeeping, the rest should be fairly important for every player.

Ball control

Different parts of the foot can be used for controlling the ball, such as the inside, the outside, the sole, and the instep. The ball can be played directly toward a player in a stationary position and then to either side of him. The more proficient a player becomes with this technique, the wider the ball can be placed.

Cushioning the Ball

The controlling surface is withdrawn on impact to absorb the pace of the ball. If a ball has to be controlled out of the air, the player should attempt to get the ball down to the feet as quickly as possible in order to perform the next technique. The chest, thigh, and foot are the parts of the body used most frequently in controlling a ball.

Chest

This is the largest area of the body and can be likened to a large pillow or a cushion that absorbs whatever hits it. The surface is immediately withdrawn as the ball touches the chest so as to cushion and therefore prevent the ball from rebounding out of control.

Thigh

There is more of a cushioning effect with this part of the body due to the muscle mass in contact with the ball. The actual part of the thigh that is used can be marked approximately at the bottom of the player's shorts.

Foot

Different parts of the foot can be used successfully depending upon what the player's next move will be.

— *Inside*: This is the largest area of the foot and the most frequently used. A beginning player will make this surface the only form of control even though it has the major disadvantage of breaking the stride pattern if the player is attempting to control the ball while moving. This is due to the awkward position of the foot, which must be turned outward to receive the ball in balance.

— *Outside*: Beginning players should be encouraged to use this part of the foot because of its effectiveness in setting up the ball for a drive pass or a shot. The ball can be squeezed to the outside of the player's body with very little effort of foot readjustment. This is done with a smooth movement which can also disguise the player's intentions to a defender. However, some players do have difficulty making the slight adjustment needed to push the ball out to the side and out in front. They will usually overplay one of the other.

— *Instep*: This is normally used when a ball is dropping and the player has time to control without interference from the opposition. It can also be used when moving in stride to take the pace off the ball without completely bringing the ball to a stop.

— *Sole:* Use of this part of the foot is often referred to as the wedge trap: the ball is wedged between the sole of the foot and the ground. However, with the ball stopped in this manner, defenders can close in quickly and force the player with the ball to react too quickly in making his next move. Beginning players will use this form of control to line up for the push pass.

Passing and Receiving

Soccer is a team game. Passing and receiving are probably the most vital skills that a player can have. These skills help to link a team together and form the essence of teamwork. Poor passing and receiving skills will eventually lead to loss of possession and wastes scoring opportunities.

There are many different ways to pass and receive a ball. Here we are going to teach you how to pass and receive ground and lofted balls. This guide will be divided into two sections, one concerning ground balls and the other concerning lofted balls.

Passing Ground Balls

The three basic techniques of passing ground balls are: inside of foot, outside of foot and the instep pass. Which technique you choose to use will depend on the situation you are in.

Inside-of-Foot Pass

This basic passing skill is commonly called the push pass. This is usually used to cover a distance of 3 to 13 metres. These are the steps:

— Face your target

— Approach the ball and plant your balance foot beside the ball.

— Position kicking foot after swinging your foot back.

— Swing kicking foot forward and contact the centre of the ball with the inside surface of your foot.

— Use momentum to push the ball forward.

— Have a smooth follow-through.

Outside-of-Foot Pass

This passing technique is usually employed while you are dribbling and want to pass the ball diagonally. This pass is more deceptive and less predictable.

— Face your target.

— Approach the ball and plant your balance foot behind and to the side of the ball.

— Bend kicking foot back at the knee.

— Snap the foot inside out with your foot rotated slightly inwards.

— Contact the ball with the outside surface of your foot.

— For longer passes use a complete follow-through.

Instep Pass

The instep pass is used to cover a distance of 20 metres or greater. The 'instep' is the portion of your foot covered by your shoelaces. It is used as a hard and flat surface to hit the ball with power and accuracy.

— Approach the ball at a slight angle.

— Place your non-kicking foot beside the ball.

— Kick the ball, and allow your leg to continue moving upwards, even after you have kicked the ball.

This is called the follow-through and it provides more power to your shot. When you limit your follow-through, you force your leg to stop after the ball flies. This movement cannot be precisely calculated and often the result is a rather weak shot.

Receiving Ground Balls

Depending on the situation, you have a choice of using either your inside or outside of foot to receive the ball. In both instances, you must withdraw the receiving surface as the ball hits to cushion the impact. Failure in cushioning the ball will result in it bouncing away from you to another.

Inside-of-Foot Reception

— Align yourself to the incoming ball.
— Extend your receiving foot to meet the ball.
— Your receiving foot must be positioned sideways.
— Receive the ball with the inside of the foot.
— Withdraw slightly to cushion impact.

There is no need to stop the ball completely as it wastes time. Instead, direct it to the direction of your movement.

Outside-of-Foot Reception

This technique is usually used when there is an opponent nearby as you cannot use the technique above.

— Position yourself sideways to the ball.
— Preferably with your body between the opponent and the ball.
— Receive the ball with foot farthest from opponent.
— Withdraw slightly to cushion impact

Passing Lofted Balls

Sometimes a lofted pass can be a better choice than a ground pass as the may be a defender in your way. Hence you may decide to chip the ball over him to your teammate. The two basic techniques are the long chip and the short chip.

Short Chip Pass

— Approach ball from behind at an angle.
— Plant balance foot beside the ball.
— Draw back kicking foot.
— Drive it beneath the ball, contacting it below the midline with a snaplike kicking motion.
— Follow-through must be kept minimal.

Long Chip Pass

— Approach ball from behind at an angle.
— Plant balance foot behind and to the side of the ball.
— Extend kicking foot.
— Drive your instep through the lower part of the ball.
— Lean back as you contact the ball.
— Complete follow through.

Receiving Lofted Balls

The four body surfaces commonly used to receive a lofted ball are the instep, chest, thigh and head. Again, the choice depends on the trajectory of the ball.

Instep. The instep is used for receiving a ball dropping from above.

— Anticipate where the ball will fall.
— Move to the position.
— Raise your receiving foot.
— As the ball contacts, withdraw your foot to the ground to cushion the impact.

Thigh. The thigh is an alternative to receiving a dropping ball. It is normally used when under pressure from an opponent.

— Anticipate where the ball will fall.

— Move to the position.

— Raise receiving leg so the thigh is parallel to the ground.

— Flex balance leg slightly at knee.

— Receive the ball on your thigh and withdraw immediately.

— The ball should drop softly to the ground around your feet.

Chest.

— Face the oncoming ball.

— Arch your upper body slightly backward.

— Receive ball on the central area of your chest.

— Withdraw your upper body as the ball arrives to cushion impact.

— Women are allowed to cross their arms against their chests to receive such balls. However many do not usually do so.

Head.

— Position under dropping ball.

— Jump upward with both feet.

— Angle head backward.

— Contact the ball on your forehead at the highest point of your jump.

— The ball should bounce off slightly to land near your feet.

DRILLS

Passing Drills

Off the Wall

Position yourself with the ball three metres from a wall. Use the inside of foot pass to rebound the ball off the wall. Receive the rebounds and pass again. Try to pass and receive the ball 20 of 25 times without error. Use either inside or outside of foot passing and receiving techniques.

Long Distance Passing and Receiving

Stand 20 to 25 metres apart with a partner. Use the instep or long chip technique to pass the ball back and forth. Receive the ball using the various techniques. Try to accurately pass and receive the ball 10 of 15 times.

Shooting Drills

Dead-ball shooting

Set up an outline of a goal on a wall. Use the instep drive technique to shoot a stationary ball at the goal from about 15 metres out. Collect the rebound and pick a different spot to shoot from.

Take 20 shots with each foot. A point is awarded for each shot on target (in the goal) and the aim is to get 32 out of 40 points.

To increase the difficulty:

— Increase the distance
— Make the goal smaller
— Try a swerving shot instead of a normal instep drive

First-timing the ball

You need at least 3 people for this activity. One of your teammates plays as goalkeeper. You position yourself 25 metres from goal, and the third player will be 15 metres away from goal, directly in front of you.

Pass to the third player. He will push pass it lightly to the side (either side will do). Sprint forward and shoot the ball first-time (meaning without stopping the ball beforehand). Take rebounds, if any.

Rotate players after each shot, and repeat the drill. Play until each player has completed 30 shots at goal. Award 1 point for a shot on target — forcing the goalkeeper to make a save — and 2 points for a goal. Your aim is to get at least 40 out of 60 points.

Toss and Volley

Position yourself 25 metres away from goal. Get someone to be the goalkeeper. Toss a ball upwards so that it will drop in front of you. Allow the ball to bounce once, then volley it. Use all three different types of volleys — the full volley, half volley and side volley. Do not practice the overhead volley with this drill. Try each volley 10 times.

Award yourself a point for a shot on target, and 2 for a goal. The aim here is to get 14 points out of 20 for the full volleys, 12/20 for the half volleys and 10/20 for the side volleys.

Goalkeeping Drills

Distributing by hand

Distribute the ball to a partner using:

— Rolling: 10 metres away
— Baseball Throw: 25 metres away

— Javelin Throw: 35 metres away (Repeat each drill 20 times)

Throws are considered accurate when your partner does not have to move more than 3 metres (in any direction) to get to the ball. For rolling balls, 18 out of 20 should be accurate, while for baseball throws, 15/20 are expected to be accurate. For javelin throws, 12 out of 20 accurate throws is a good target to aim for.

Handling the ball

Hold the ball at chest level. Bounce it off the ground and catch it with your hands in the the W position before it goes above the waist. Do it 40 times, aiming to catch and hold 36 out of 40.

Saving the ball

Three servers position themselves an equal distance apart, along the 6-yard line in front of goal. Go [in goal]. Server 1 at the corner of the [6-yard box] will roll a ball which you receive, and return. Move to server 2, who will toss the ball at chest level to you. Receive and return. The third server will toss a high ball to you, which you will catch and return. You should continue until 30 balls have been thrown at you, 26 of which you should have caught.

Forward-vault saves

Your partner standing about 5 metres away from you will bounce you a ball. Vault forward to receive the ball, and bounce it back to your partner to allow him to practice as well. Try it 20 times, and see if you can catch and hold at least 15.

Standing dive saves

A team-mate about 5 metres away serves you a rolling

ball or waist high ball a few metres off to either side. Dive to save the ball. Try ten saves for each side, aiming to catch and hold seven of those.

Setpieces Drills

Free Kicks

Free kicks outside of scoring distance should be played as quickly as possible before the defense can organize. Free kicks closer to the goal often have sophisticated plays associated with them. The options are to shoot directly at goal, play the ball over the defensive wall or pass around the wall.

The player or players who are designated to take the free kicks should practise kicking long hard balls for far kicks and chip shots for balls kicked over a defensive wall. For the remainder of the team,drills consist of practicing over and over where they should go and what they should do in each situation. Each team and each coach will have different plays for their team and so it is important to keep practicing them.

Practice makes perfect and each play should be rehearsed thoroughly during practice so that play selection, signaling and execution are precise in game play. Plays can start being practiced with only the offensive players and goalie involved and can intensify with more and more defensive players being added.

There is no special defensive tactic for free kicks when the ball is far from the goal and cannot be played directly into the goal area. The defending team moves quickly to get between the ball and goal. When a kick is taken close to the scoring area, the defense usually forms a wall to block the path to the goal. The purpose of the wall at closer distances is to protect the near half of the goal. The goalie covers the far half of the goal. The number of people in the wall depends on the distance of the kick from goal and the angle. Usually the goalie positions the wall, telling them to move right or left.

There are many different free kick plays and so it is important to assign different roles and responsibilities to individual players. There are no specific drills one can use to learn how to defend against free kicks. Usually teams start with only offensive players practicing free kick plays and then they add defensive players to the practice. The most important thing players must learn in practicing defense against free kicks is who will have what role.

Corner Kicks

As with free kicks the only drill for a team to practice is a repetition of the plays they have set up for corner kicks. Plays can be make nearly perfect through practicing proper technique, communication, movement and timing. It is important for the person taking the corner kicks to be able to place the ball exactly where each play demands and it is important for all the other players to know exactly what role they assume for each of their teams plays. Once again, as with free kicks, most teams start practicing their corner kick plays with only offensive players and an opposing goalie and then gradually add defensive players to make the drill more like a real game situation.

When the opposing team is awarded a corner kick, you are already in your defensive third of the field. Although how the offensive team sets up determines a lot of how the defense sets up, there is usually a partially prearranged defensive setup that the players must be able to quickly move to.

Often, two defensive players will position themselves near the far post- one to protect the space behind the goalkeeper and the other to move out to cover an attacker who has occupied or is attempting to occupy vulnerable space. The goalkeeper will typically be close enough to the far post to be able to intercept a long cross to the far post or to move along the goal line or forward away from the goal line to catch balls that swing in toward the goal. A defender will probably be at the near post to clear a short kick from the goal area or to pass the ball to a teammate. Usually, another defender will be 10 yards from the player taking the corner kick to provide distraction and to be in position to intercept an errant cross or a pass to a nearby attacker.

Other defensive players usually mark attacking players who have moved or may move to scoring positions. Defenders will try to create depth by positioning players from the goal line out to the middle third of the field so that a defender can clear or pass the ball immediately upfield to a teammate.

It is important for the team to practice their defensive strategy over and over so that in a game situation, each players knows exactly where to go and what to do. Players must also be able to read each situation and adapt their behaviour accordingly. Communication is a key so that each defender knows what the others are doing.

Heading

Generally, players use their foreheads when heading a ball. This is a very hard part of the head which permits painless contact with the ball, when proper heading techniques are used, can project the ball with considerable velocity and accuracy.

— Keep eyes on the ball at all times.

— As ball approaches bend knees slightly.

— Placing one foot behind other, rock back, transferring weight onto back legs.
— Keep arms out for balance.
— Arch upper body back, then snap upper body, neck, and head forward as ball contacts the forehead.
— Transfer weight to front leg on contact.
— Drive head "through" ball. Follow through for maximum power.

Jump Heading

Both attacking and defending players must be able to head the ball while in the air. Especially in front of the goal, attackers will often be called on to jump and head in an attempt to score, while defenders do the same in an attempt to get the ball out from in front of their goal. Players who are poor ball headers will invariably find themselves at a great disadvantage on these occasions in every match.

When jump heading, always keep eyes on ball, head from the hips, not just by waffling the head itself. Power stems from the waist and from the legs, time your spring when jumping to head.

Offensive Heading

Get over top of the ball and head it down, it's harder for the goalie to save a ball on the ground than one right to his hands.

Defensive Heading

Head the ball in the air, away from danger.

Shooting

Poor finishing is a major reason why most teams that look good on paper flop on the turf. Teams can create chances — that's an important part of attacking play — but if the chances are not converted into goals then it is entirely useless. In soccer, the players easiest to remember, most of the time, are the goalscorers. It is the player who gets the goals who gets the credit most of the time.

Instep Drive

The instep drive shot is used to strike a rolling or stationary ball. The technique used is similar to that of the instep pass, except that the follow-through here is greater.

— Approach the ball at a slight angle.

— Place your non-kicking foot beside the ball.

— Kick the ball, and allow your leg to continue moving upwards, even after you have kicked the ball.

This is called the follow-through and it provides more power to your shot. When you limit your follow-through, you force your leg to stop after the ball flies. This movement cannot be precisely calculated and often the result is a rather weak shot.

Volleying the ball

Volleying the ball is used when the ball is in midair. Difficult to execute, volleys require precise timing and correct technique. The four different kinds of volley are the full volley, half volley, side volley and overhead volley.

Full Volley

— Move to where the ball is about to drop.

— Face the ball with your shoulders squared.

— Extend arms to the sides to keep balance.

— Kick the dropping ball.
— Complete the follow-through.

Half Volley

Similar to the full volley, the half volley is executed when the ball touches the ground, rather than when in midair as with the full volley.

— Move to where the ball is about to drop.
— Face the ball with your shoulders squared.
— Extend arms to keep balance.
— Kick the ball as it touches the ground.
— Complete the follow-through.

Side Volley

Used when the ball is bouncing at your side, the side volley is quite difficult to execute as it requires precise timing and a good sense of balance.

— Raise kicking leg by the side, parallel to ground.
— Draw back kicking leg, bending at the knee.
— Extend kicking leg, keeping weight on balancing foot.
— Front shoulder should be facing target.
— Kick the top half of the ball with your instep.
— Follow through, angling the kick slightly downwards.
— Drop kicking foot towards ground.

Overhead Volley

Considered the most spectacular and naturally the most dangerous of the volleys, the overhead volley hinges on precise timing.

— (While the ball is still high above you) Turn to make your back face the intended target.
— Watch the ball descend.
— When it is about head level, jump.
— In a scissors-like motion, kick the air beside of the ball with your non-kicking foot, then kick the ball with your kicking foot.

This, if executed well, makes for a great goal, while if it is badly done, could cause a bad back injury.

Swerving Shot

The most direct path to goal is not always the best. Shots that swerve in flight are difficult to catch, and might fool the most experienced of keepers. A swerving shot is executed in the following manner:

— Approach ball from behind and plant balancing foot beside the ball.
— Extend arms out to sides to keep balance.
— With the instep or the outside of the kicking foot, hit the ball either left or right of the vertical midline.
— Kick hard.
— Follow through to waist level or higher.

Goalkeeping

The goalkeeper is undoubtably the most important and unique player on the soccer field. Besides being the only player legally able to use his hands on the field, the goalkeeper is straddled with the responsibility to save his team from the jaws of defeat or keep his team on the road to victory.

As a goalkeeper, one must be able to catch or block all shots directed at one's goal. Besides being the last line of defense, a keeper is also responsible for starting your

team's attack by distributing the ball accurately. The goalkeeper position is a demanding one, both physically and mentally.

Goalkeeping skills you can pick up from SGO include the basic stance, methods of receiving high, low, and middle shots, how to dive well, and how to distribute the ball.

Basic Stance

The basic goalkeeping stance is assumed when an opponent has the ball within shooting range. This position allows easy movement in all directions.

Square your shoulders to the ball, with feet spread shoulder width apart. Your head and upper body must remain straight and knees slightly flexed. Body weight should be centred on the balls of your feet, with heels slightly above the ground. Position your hips and behind as if you were sitting on a medium-height bar stool. Hold hands at about waist level, with palms forward and fingers pointing upwards. Keep your head steady and focus on the ball.

Distribution of the Ball

After a save is made, play has to resume, and this is done by the goalkeeper passing the ball out. When the intended target is less than 15 metres away, you may want to roll the ball to him or her. This is just like bowling; keep the ball on the floor. Throwing the ball is another option. Throws can be classified into two main types, the "baseball throw" and the "javelin throw", both of which resemble their namesakes. The javelin throw is naturally more powerful as it involves the entire throwing arm rather than only the hand. Of course, the most powerful way, though not always the most accurate, is to kick the ball upfield. The full volley punt and the drop kick are two of the common methods used by keepers around the world. Both are about the same; you chuck the ball into the air and volley it upfield. Only difference is, with the full volley punt, a full volley is used, while with the drop kick, it is a half volley. The drop kick is preferably used on windy days.

Saving Low Shots

Ball rolling directly at keeper

— Assume ready position.

— Bend forward at waist, with arms extended downwards, palms forward and cupped.

— Allow ball to roll onto wrist and forearm.

— Withdraw slightly upon impact (holding ball) and return to standing position.

— Distribute the ball. You may choose to clutch the ball to your chest first to signal to the opposing forwards that it is now out of bounds to them.

Handling

Saving the Ball

— Low shot directly at keeper

— Assume ready position.

— Bend forward at the waist, with knees flexed.

— Dive forward with arms extended towards ball.

— Scoop ball up and drop onto forearms. Keep the ball between your chest and arms.

— Spread your legs and get to your feet.

— Distribute the ball.

Forward-vault Save

— Ball rolling to side of keeper
— Assume ready position.
— Shuffle across goal towards the ball.
— Extend lead foot, flex knee.
— Kneel on trailing leg.
— Follow steps 2 to 5 of the "ball rolling directly at keeper" technique.

Saving high balls

— Chest-high or head-high shots
— Assume ready position.
— Watch the ball as it arrives.
— Stretch arms out to catch it, with hands in a "W" position.
— With arms flexed, look through the "window".
— Receive ball on fingertips and withdraw on contact to soften the impact of the ball.
— Distribute the ball.

Overhead shots

— Assume ready position. Move towards the ball.
— Jump, taking off on one leg.
— Extend arms, with hands in a "W" position.
— Head behind your hands.
— Catch the ball at the peak of your jump.
— Distribute the ball.

Diving to make a save

One of the most acrobatic and exciting moments in soccer

is when a goalkeeper dives across goal to deny the opposing team their point.

— Assume ready position.
— Jump, pushing off with the foot in the direction you wish to dive; ie the right foot for for a dive to the right.
— Extend your arms. Keep your head behind your arms.
— Receive the ball with your fingertips and palms, or punch it away.
— If you have the ball, clutch it to your chest.
— Fall on your side, not your stomach, to prevent injury.

Defending

The defender is one who cannot afford to take risks when attempting to win the ball. This is because one small mistake could result in a goal for the opponent, especially if the culprit is the last man in defence. Thus, a defender's main objective is to keep the opponent in front of you and prevent telling passes or penetrating dribbles from being made.

One-on-One

Goalside positioning

Always position yourself goal-side, between the opponent you are marking and your goal post. This shuts off the most direct route to goal for the attacker and gives you a good view at all times.

Approach the ball

Close the distance between yourself and the opponent when he is about to receive the ball. slow down as you reach him to maintain your balance and control.

Defensive stance

Assume a slight crouched position with your knees flexed. From this position, somewhat like the goalkeeper's ready position, you can easily move in any direction. Position your legs in a staggered stance with one leg ahead of the other, which saves you from being nutmegged.

Preventing the turn

Try to prevent the opponent from turning with the ball to face your goal, as he can pass or dribble on.

Tackle the ball, not the legs

When you feel that you have allowed the opponent with the ball to get too far away, get in close, then tackle hard to gain position of the ball. Do not overcommit in the effort as you may be beaten on the dribble.

Tackling Skills

Block Tackle

— Close the distance and assume defensive stance.
— Draw blocking foot and position it sideways.
— Face the dribbler, shoulders squared.
— Move momentum forward and drive blocking foot through the ball.
— Keep your foot firm as you push the ball forward past the opponent.
— When you have possession, initiate the counterattack.

Poke Tackle

— Close the distance and assume the defensive stance.

- — Extend tackling foot.
- — Flex balance leg.
- — Poke the ball with your toes.
- — Withdraw leg to avoid contact with dribbler.
- — Chase and regain possession of the ball.

Slide Tackle

- — Approaching from the side, slide on your side with your arms extended out to the sides for balance.
- — Extend lower leg, with your upper leg flexed at the knee.
- — Use the instep of the lower leg to hit the ball away.
- — Try to avoid dribbler.
- — Jump to feet and collect the ball if possible.

SETPIECES

Free Kicks

Type A

Formation. The ball is placed 10 yards outside the middle of the 18-yard line. Attacker 1 is in position to take the free kick, Attacker 2 is five yards to the right of 1 and Attacker 3 is five yards to the right of 2.

Procedure. 2 runs toward the near-post end of the defensive wall. 1 passes to 3, who takes a first-time shot on goal.

Type B

Formation. The ball is placed just outside the right corner of the penalty area. Attackers 1 and 2 are in position to take the free kick. Attacker 3 takes a weak-side position even with, and about 20 yards to the side of, the defensive wall.

Procedure. 1 fakes a shot on goal and runs over the ball aroud the near-post side of the wall, staying onside. In rapid sequence, 2 passes to 3, who has made a timed run toward the wall, and 3 makes a one-touch pass behind the wall to 1 who takes a shot on goal.

Type C

Formation. The ball is placed outside the right side of the 18-yard line. Attackers 1, 2, and 3 are in position to take the free kick. Attackers 4, 5, and 6 are in a line along the far left side of the 18-yard line.

Procedure. In sequence, 1 runs over the ball and makes a curling run toward the penalty line, 2 runs over the ball and makes a straight run past the near-post end of the wall, and 4, 5, and 6 run toward the far post. 3 makes a chip pass to the far post, and either 4, 5, or 6 takes a one time head shot on goal. The runs and pass must be timed to avoid players off the ball getting into offside positions.

Corner Kicks

Type 1

Formation. Attacker 1 is in position to take the corner kick. Attackers 2 and 3 are on the far sideline of the goal area. Attackers 4, 5, and 6 are in a line 15 yards from the goal line and parallel to the 18-yard line.

Procedure. To initiate the restart play and to distract the goalkeeper, 2 and 3 sprint across the goal area and curl back once they reach the near sideline of the goal area. 4, 5, and 6 check in the direction of 1 and then curl back toward the goal area-4 toward the far post, 5 to the middle, and 6 toward the near post. 4, as the main target, must make an effective feinting move to get open. 1 counts one second and makes the corner kick to 4, who takes a first-time shot on goal. All other attackers stay alert for a possible rebound.

Type 2

Formation. Attacker 1 is in a position to take the corner kick. Attackers 2 and 3 are at the near corner of the goal area. Attackers 4, 5, and 6 are next to each other at the far corner of the penalty area. Attacker 7 is at the midpoint of the penalty-area restraining arc.

Procedure. On a predetermined signal from 1, 2 runs toward the near sideline of the penalty area. 1 makes the corner kick to 2's head. 5 sprints to the middle of the goal area,and 6 sprints toward the far post. 2 flicks to 3 or 5. Whoever contacts the ball takes a first-time shot on goal. 6 stays alert for a possible rebound of a further flick from 5. 4 and 7 stay alert for a possible long rebound or defensive clear.

Type 3

Formation. Attacker 1 is in position to take the corner kick. Attacker 2 is at the near-post corner of the goal area. Attackers 3, 4, 5, and 6 stand from left to right along th top of th 18-yard line.

Procedure. 1 initiates the corner kick by giving a predetermined signal to 2. 2 moves toward 1. 1 plays a short ball to 2 at the penalty area sideline and receives a pass back from 2. As 2 makes the pass, the attackers on the 18-yard line sprint into the goal area, with 3 and 6 crisscrossing to the far and near posts, respectively, and 4 and 5 making straight runs. 1 either takes a shot on goal or passes to one of the attackers in the goal area, who takes a shot on goal. All other attackers stay alert for a possible rebound.

DRIBBLING

To the spectator this part of the game can be as artistic as a well-executed shot on goal. By being able to master the ball with the feet in tight situations a player can place the opposition at a disadvantage through taking away the numerical superiority defenders usually have.

Many qualities are essential to dribbling, including pace, strength, stamina and determination, but balance is vital. It enables them to ride tackles and still get through. It enables them to evade unfair challenges, to retain possession when the odds are against them. Use any part of your body for holding off challenges, your hips, shoulders, buttocks or your arms to ward of defenders.

The object of the dribbler will be to set the defender up, get him off balance, unsettle him and then leave him behind. Some players will aim to defeat their opponent by a sudden movement of the body.

A change of direction must be followed immediately by a change of pace. Defenders will recover from mistakes quickly, and therefore it is important for an accelerated phase to accompany the change in direction. Continuing at the same pace will allow the defender to challenge a second time.

All players should be inventive, creative, and prepared to take risks. The ability to take on and beat other players by dribbling is a positive attribute for a player to possess.

6

American Football

American football, known in the United States and Canada simply as football, is a competitive team sport known for its physical roughness despite being a highly strategic game. The object of the game is to score points by advancing the prolate spheroid ball into the opposing team's end zone. The ball can be advanced by carrying it (a running play) or by throwing it to a teammate (a passing play). Points can be scored in a variety of ways, including carrying the ball over the goal line, throwing the ball to another player past the goal line or kicking it through the goal posts on the opposing side. The winner is the team with the most points when the time expires and the last play ends.

Outside the United States and Canada, the sport is referred to as American football (or a translation thereof) to differentiate it from other football games. In Australia and New Zealand the game is known as Gridiron, although in America the word "gridiron" refers only to the playing field.

The Gallup Poll has shown football to be America's favorite sport every year since 1972, when football first overtook baseball in popularity. The percentage of Americans who say football is their favorite sport to watch (43%) is higher now than at any other time. Football's American TV viewership ratings far surpass those of other sports. The day of the National Football League championship, the Super Bowl, is one of the biggest occasions for social gatherings in the U.S. and is sometimes referred to as an unofficial national holiday.

College football is also popular throughout North America. Four college football stadiums, The University of Michigan's Michigan Stadium, Penn State's Beaver Stadium, The University of Tennessee's Neyland Stadium and Ohio State's Ohio Stadium, seat more than 100,000 fans and almost always sell out. Even high school football games can attract more than 10,000 people in some areas. The weekly autumn ritual of college and high-school football-which includes marching bands, cheerleaders, homecoming, and parties (including the ubiquitous tailgate party)-is an important part of the culture in much of smalltown America. Football is generally the major source of revenue to the athletic programs of schools, public and private, in the United States. Some private Christian High Schools even play for 'national championships' with groups like the Federated Christian Athletic Association (FCAA).

It is a long-standing tradition in the United States (though not universally observed) that high school football games are played on Friday night, college games on Saturday, and professional games on Sunday, with one NFL game played on Monday night. In recent years, however, nationally televised Thursday night college games have become a weekly fixture on ESPN.

Certain fall and winter holidays-most notably Thanksgiving and New Year's Day-have traditional football games associated with them.

Football is played recreationally by amateur and youth teams (e.g., the Pop Warner little-league programs). There are also many "semi-pro" teams in leagues where the players are paid to play but at a small enough salary that they generally must also hold a full-time job. Organized football is played almost exclusively by men and boys, although a few amateur and semi-professional women's leagues have begun play in recent years.

The NFL operated a developmental league, NFL Europa, with teams in five German cities and one in the Netherlands, but this league folded following the 2007 season. The professional Canadian Football League and collegiate Canadian Interuniversity Sport play under Canadian rules. The sport is popular as an amateur activity in Mexico and American Samoa and to a lesser extent in Japan, Europe, Korea, The Bahamas, Chile, Brazil, Uruguay, Argentina, Australia (Gridiron Australia), Israel and the United Kingdom (BAFL). The International Federation of American Football is the governing body for American football with 45 member associations from North and South America, Europe, Asia and Oceania. The IFAF also oversees the American Football World Cup, which is held every four years. Japan won the first two World Cups, held in 1999 and 2003. Team USA, which had not participated in the previous World Cups, won the title in 2007. Despite this, the game has been slow to catch on in most countries.

History

Both American football and soccer have their origins in varieties of football played in the United Kingdom in the mid-19th century. American football is directly descended from rugby football. The majority of the plays in a typical American football game involve handling the ball rather than kicking it.

Many "first" American football games have been claimed. However, many such games were played under rules that were so different from today's game as to call into question the veracity of the claims. The origins of

American football probably date to the early 1800s when teams from various colleges and secondary schools (necessarily from the Eastern part of the United States because established institutions of learning existed only in that region at the time) met to attempt to move an inflated ball past a line to gain points. This movement was usually achieved by kicking or batting at the ball, as in soccer. The number of men on each side (as men were only then allowed to compete) was quite different than the eleven which characterizes the modern game. As to the 'first' game of American football, it has been claimed that Rutgers University and Princeton University played the first game of college football on Nov. 6, 1869 in New Brunswick, New Jersey, won by Rutgers 6-4. However, the viewpoint that this particular game marks the beginning of American football is contested.

The English Football (i.e., Soccer) Association rules were followed in the Princeton/Rutgers contest; participants were only allowed to kick the ball; and each side had twenty five men. Some see the Princeton/ Rutgers meeting of 1869 as the first intercollegiate game of "soccer" in America, but not American football Dartmouth College students played a football-like game now known as "Old Division Football," to which they published rules in 1871. If one must require that there be a starting point, or "first" game, of American football between two American teams, that distinction would have to go to the contest played between Tufts University and Harvard University on June 4, 1875 at Jarvis Field in Cambridge, Mass., won by Tufts 1-0

Jarvis Field was at the time located off Massachusetts Avenue in Cambridge, between Everett and Jarvis Sts. which bordered the northern point of the Harvard campus. A report of the outcome of this game appeared in the Boston Daily Globe of June 5, 1875. In the Tufts/ Harvard game participants were allowed to pick up the ball and run with it, each side fielded eleven men, the ball carrier was stopped by knocking him down or "tackling" him, and the inflated ball was egg-shaped - the combination of which far more closely resembles the modern American football game than the games of other "firsts". Thus, the Harvard/Tufts game may be regarded as the beginning of football between two American colleges. It should also be noted that a year prior to the Tufts/Harvard game, Harvard faced McGill University of Montreal, Canada on May 14, 1874 in a game under rules similar to the Tufts/Harvard game. This marks the Harvard/McGill game as the first game of football in "North" America. To this day, Harvard, McGill and Tufts continue to field football teams though they no longer play each other.

Encouraged by Yale University's Walter Camp, the schools began to adopt more standardized rules that would differentiate American football from rugby in the 1880s. The scrimmage was introduced in 1880 and the system of downs in 1882.

By the turn of the 20th century, football had become notoriously dangerous; 18 college players died in 1905 alone. Colleges responded with a series of rule changes to open up the game, most importantly the forward pass, along with outlawing dangerous formations such as the "flying wedge", and introducing and requiring better equipment such as helmets.

The game had achieved its modern form by 1912, when the field was changed to its current size, the value of a touchdown increased to 6 points, and a fourth down added to each possession. Originally dominated by the Ivy League, football soon captured the interest of colleges nationwide. By 1916, when the Rose Bowl game matching eastern and western teams became an annual event, football had developed a national following second only to baseball among team sports.

Professional football developed in the mill towns of Pennsylvania and the American Midwest in the early years of the 20th century. The NFL was founded in 1920 in Canton, Ohio as the American Professional Football Association; it adopted its current name in 1922. Professional football remained a largely regional sport of secondary importance until after World War II, when television broadcasts boosted NFL football's national appeal. The pro game surpassed both college football and baseball in popularity in the 1960s. The first Super Bowl-between the champions of the NFL and the rival American Football League-was played in 1967, and the leagues merged in 1970.

American Football Rules

Game play in American football consists of a series of individual plays of short duration, outside of which the ball is dead or not in play. These can be plays from scrimmage-passes, runs, punts, and field goal attempts-or free kicks such as kickoffs. Substitutions can be made between plays, which allows for a great deal of specialization as coaches choose the players best suited for each particular situation. During a play, each team should have 11 players on the field, and each of them usually have specific tasks assigned for that specific play.

Object of the Game

The object of the game is to score points by advancing the ball to the opponent's end zone for a touchdown, or to kick field goals, and to prevent the other team from doing likewise. The team with the most points when time has expired wins.

Time of Play

Collegiate and professional football games are 60 minutes long, divided into four quarters of 15 minutes each. In high school football, 12 minute quarters are usually played. The clock is stopped frequently, however, so that a typical professional game can exceed three hours in duration. Timing is stopped after any incomplete pass and any play that ends out of bounds (although in the NFL the clock restarts on the referee's ready-for-play signal outside the last two minutes of the first half and the last five minutes of the second half). In addition, each team is allowed 3 timeouts each half that they may use at their discretion.

The clock may also be stopped for an officials' time-out, after which, if the clock was running, it is restarted. For example; if there is a question as to whether or not a team has moved the ball far enough for a first down, the officials may bring the chains in to measure. While this measurement is taking place, the officials will signal for a stoppage of the clock. Once the measurement is finished and the ball is spotted, the referee will then signal for the clock to restart. Additional situations where officials make take a time-out are to administer a penalty and for an injured player to be removed from the field.

In addition to the game clock, a secondary play clock is also usually displayed. This counts down the time the offense has to start the next play before it is assessed a delay of game penalty.

Officials call for media time-outs after a change of possession (turnover by interception, fumble or on downs), following a successful PAT (Point(s) After Touchdown) or a field goal try, or in the NFL after a kickoff when the opposing team scored, usually when there is more than 5 minutes to play in each quarter. If an instant replay challenge is called during the game, the referees also signal for a media time out. The referee signals these media time-outs by first using the time out signal, then extending both arms in a horizontal position.

Separating the second and third quarters is a halftime. Teams change ends of the field at the end of the first quarter and the end of the third quarter. In the NFL, an automatic timeout is called by the officials when there are two minutes left (or less than two minutes if the play began with over two minutes left and ended with less than two minutes left) in both the second and the fourth quarters; this is most commonly referred to as the two-minute warning. No such warning is normally given in amateur football, though if there is no visible stadium clock, the referee will give a two-minute warning (four minutes in high school).

Overtime

If a game is tied at the end of four quarters, overtime is played.

In the NFL, overtime periods are 15 minutes in length and are sudden death, meaning that the team that scores first, by any means, wins, and the game automatically ends (referred to in recent years as a walk-off touchdown, walk-off field goal or in rare situations, a walk-off safety). A coin flip is employed to determine which team will gain possession first; the winning team has the option to either receive the kickoff or choose the side of the field they wish to defend. During the regular season in the NFL, one overtime period is played (with each team receiving two time outs), and if neither team scores during overtime, the game officially ends in a tie. In the playoffs, as many overtimes are played as are necessary to determine a winner.

The longest professional football game in history was played in 1984 between the Los Angeles Express and the Michigan Panthers of the now-defunct USFL; with the Express winning the game 27-21 after 3:33 of the third overtime period at the Los Angeles Memorial Coliseum.

NFL Europa, a developmental league run by the NFL, uses a 10-minute overtime period, with the constraint that each team must have the opportunity of possession; once both teams have had such an opportunity, the overtime proceeds in a manner similar to the NFL's. Thus, if Team A has the first possession of overtime and scores a touchdown and converts their kick (thus being 7 points ahead of Team B), Team A would then kick off to Team B (In the NFL, the game would have ended with the touchdown, without a conversion being attempted). Team B would have to match or exceed the 7 point difference within this ensuing possession; exceeding it would end the game immediately, while matching the difference would result in a kickoff to Team A. From this point, the overtime is sudden death.

In college and high school football, an overtime procedure (the Kansas plan) ensures that each team has equal opportunity to score. In college, both teams are granted possession of the ball at their opponents' 25 yard-line in succession. A coin flip takes place, with the winning team having the option either 1) to declare that they will take the ball first or second, or 2) to decide on which end of the field the series will occur (both teams' series occur on the same end of the field).

The losing team will have the first option in any subsequent even-numbered overtime. In the first overtime, the team with first series attempts to score either a touchdown or a field goal; their possession ends when either a touchdown or a field goal have been scored, they turn the ball over via a fumble or an interception, or they fail to gain a first down. After a touchdown, a team may attempt either an extra-point or a two-point conversion. (However, if the team on defense during the first series recovers a fumble and returns it for a touchdown, or returns an interception for a touchdown, the defensive team wins the game. This is the only way for a college overtime game to end without both teams having possession.) Regardless of the outcome of the first team's series (be it touchdown, field goal, or turnover), the other team begins their series. If the score remains tied after both teams have completed a series, a second overtime begins. If the score remains tied after two overtimes, teams scoring touchdowns are required to attempt a two-point conversion from the third overtime on. Just as in regulation, if a defensive team recovers a fumble/returns an interception to the end zone during a two-point conversion attempt, they will receive two points.

In high school football, in most of the states, each team is granted possession of the ball at the 10-yard line, meaning that a team cannot make a first down without scoring except via a defensive penalty that carries an automatic first down. As is the case with the college overtime rule, the team that wins the coin toss will have the choice as to whether to take the ball first or second, or decide at which end of the field the overtime will be played. The other major difference between overtime in college football and high school football is that in high school football, if the defense forces a turnover, they may not score. However, in Texas, the college overtime rule is used, as the University Interscholastic League, which governs interscholastic activities for Texas public high schools, plays by NCAA football rules with a few modifications for the high school level.

Playing the Game

Coin toss

The game begins with a kickoff, which is one type of free kick. Prior to the game, captains from each team participate in a coin toss. The winner of the toss may make one of the following choices: to kickoff, to receive and have the other team kickoff, or to choose an end of the field to defend. The toss winner nearly always chooses to receive, because that means they get to go first on offense. The other team then may choose from the remaining options (usually which end of the field to defend). In amateur football, the winner of the toss may also defer their choice to the second half and give the other team first choice of options in the first half. This is typically done when the captain winning the toss wants to receive to start the second half.

A kickoff is also used to start the second half of the game. The team who did not get first choice at the coin toss now chooses; likewise, they nearly always choose to receive. Kickoffs also take place after each touchdown and field goal, with the scoring team kicking off.

Kickoffs

The ball is placed on a tee (or held) at the kicking team's 30 yard line (35 yard line in college and 40 for high school). The kicking team's players line up on the field parallel to and behind this line and may not cross it until the ball is kicked. A valid kickoff must travel at least 10 yards (though the ball is usually kicked as far as possible-40 to 70 yards), after which any player (though usually one on the receiving team) tries to catch or pick up the ball and advance it down the field before being downed. Occasionally, the kicking team may set up a kick with the intent to recover it; this onside kick is a play where the kicker tries to kick the ball just over the required 10-yard distance in a manner such that a teammate might catch it after a lucky bounce.

Receiving a kickoff

A kickoff that goes out-of-bounds anywhere other than the end zone before being touched by the receiving team results in a penalty. The receiving team may have the option to have the kicking team re-kick after a five yard penalty is enforced. Otherwise, they may choose to take the ball at the spot where it went out of bounds or 30 yards from where it was free kicked, whichever is more advantageous. Once the official places the ball after the penalty is marked off, this spot becomes the line of scrimmage. A kick that travels through the end zone, or is caught by the receiving team within the end zone but not advanced, is called a touchback. The ball is placed on the receiving team's 20 yard line, which becomes the line of scrimmage. Most commonly, however, a member of the receiving team will return the kick until he is downed. The spot of the downed ballcarrier becomes the line of scrimmage.

Downed player

A player carrying the ball (the runner) is downed when any of the following occurs:

— Any part of the runner other than the hands or feet touches the ground. This may be as a result of:

— Contact by an opponent, called down by contact, where the opponent tackles the runner by pushing him, grasping him and pulling him to the ground, sliding into his legs, or touching him in any matter that leads to any part of the runner other than the hands or feet touching the ground. Unlike the use of the word tackle in other sports, if the opposing player fails to down the ballcarrier, it is called an attempted tackle.

— Accidentally touching the ground, such as by falling. However, in professional football, the runner is not down in this situation, but may rise and continue to run unless he is down by contact, as above.

— Intentionally downing the ball: intentionally kneeling, verbally declaring "I'm down" (except in college) or similar actions. For example, to protect the quarterback from violent hits by opponents attempting to tackle him, he may slide to the ground feet-first. This slide is interpreted as intentionally downing the ball, and opponents may be penalized for hitting him.

— The runner goes out of bounds; that is, any part of his body touches anything (other than another player or an official) on or past a sideline or an endline. Note that the entire sideline is out of bounds. Note also that a runner may carry the ball such that the ball is over the sideline, but as long as the ball or runner does not touch anything out of bounds, they are deemed to be in bounds.

— The runner's forward progress toward the opponents' goal line is stopped from contact by the opponent with little chance to be resumed. The exact moment at which the player's forward progress stops may be unclear and is subject to the judgment of the officials. When this contact occurs on the quarterback, who is grasped and in the control of opponents in the backfield, the quarterback is often referred to as in the grasp.

Plays from scrimmage

The majority of a football game takes place on plays that begin at the line of scrimmage. The officials spot the ball (place it in a designated spot on the field) on the line of scrimmage and declare it ready for play.

Positions

The width of the spotted football defines the width of the neutral zone, an area of the field no player other than the snapper may position themselves in or above before the snap. Each team has its own line of scrimmage which is a vertical plane from sideline to sideline that passes through the point of the ball nearest its own goal line.

The players on offense must arrange themselves in a formation, all "behind" their line of scrimmage (that is, on the side of the line nearest their own end zone). At least seven players on offense must position themselves "on" (very near) the line; up to four may be farther from it. All players on offense must come set, or stop moving, before the snap. Once set, the offense may "shift" and come set again, as long as they do not simulate the beginning of a play. Additionally, one player at a time, called the man in motion, may be in motion, so long as he is not moving forward (toward the opponents' goal line) at the time of the snap.

The offensive linemen are the players who line up on the line. The center normally lines up directly over the ball, on each side of him is an offensive guard, and on both sides next to the guards are the offensive tackles. The rules require that 5 offensive linemen wear jerseys numbered 50-79. Usually these 5 interior lineman are the ones who wear those numbers. Any other linemen near the tackles are called tight ends and are not part of the interior line. The remaining offensive players who are called backs if they are postitioned in the backfield (the area behind the linemen), or wide receivers (also called split ends). Any wide receivers who are on the line are also linemen. The quarterback is in position to receive the ball from the center; running backs position themselves anywhere in preparation for the play; and wide receivers line up in the backfield positioned to go downfield to catch passes. Of the running backs, a halfback or a tailback will often be in position to run with the ball; a fullback will be in position to block or run with the ball.

The players on defense may arrange themselves in any manner, as long as all players are "behind the line" (that is, on the side of the line nearest their own end zone). Players who line up opposite the offensive line are called defensive linemen, usually with one or two defensive tackles in the middle and one defensive end on each side. Behind and near the linemen are positioned the linebackers; positioned opposite the wide receivers are the cornerbacks. Two other defensive players, called safeties, position themselves somewhat freely, but usually in the middle of the field behind the linebackers. These last four players are often referred to as the secondary.

Starting the Play

The play begins with a snap, where the center throws or hands the ball backward to one of the backs, usually the quarterback. The play ends when the ball is dead. The ball is typically next spotted where the ball last became dead; however, if it became dead outside the hash marks, it is brought in on the same yard line to the nearest hash mark. This spot becomes the line of scrimmage for the next play. In the case of an incomplete forward pass, the ball is returned to the spot where it was snapped to begin the previous play. A fumbled ball that goes out of bounds is declared dead and possession remains with the team that most recently had control of the ball.

Dead ball

The ball becomes dead, and the play ends, when:

— the ballcarrier is downed, as described above;

— a forward pass falls incomplete (it touches the ground before possession is secured by a player);

— the ball or ballcarrier touches the sideline or endline or otherwise goes outside the field of play ("out of bounds");

- the ballcarrier or the ball, except on a scoring field goal attempt, hits any part of the goalpost;
- a team scores;
- a kick receiver makes a fair catch (waving his arm above his head to signal a fair catch, where he the kicking team is not allowed to interfere with him or hit him after the catch, but in return he is not allowed to run), or a member of the receiving team gains possession after a fair catch signal was given;
- a member of the kicking team possesses a kicked ball (e.g. "downing" a punt allowed to roll by the receiving team by holding it to stop its roll);
- a kicked ball comes to rest;
- a touchback occurs; or
- under NFL or college rules, on fourth down, a ball fumbled forward by the offensive team is recovered by an offensive team player other than the fumbler.

The nearest official typically blows his whistle after the ball becomes dead to alert the players that the play is over. If the ball is alive and the official sounds an inadvertent whistle, then the ball still becomes dead, but the team in possession of the ball may elect to have the down replayed or take the spot where the ball was declared dead. If the ball was loose from a fumble, then the ball can be put into play at the spot of the fumble. If the ball was in flight from a kick or a pass, then the down is always replayed.

Scoring

Field goal

A field goal is scored when the ball is place kicked, drop kicked, or free kicked after a fair catch or awarded fair catch (High School or NFL only) between the goal posts behind the opponent's end zone. The most common type of kick used is the place kick. For a place kick, the ball must first be snapped to a placeholder, who holds the ball upright on the ground with his fingertip so that it may be kicked. Three points are scored if the ball crosses between the two upright posts and above the crossbar and remains over.

If a field goal is missed, the ball is returned to the original line of scrimmage (in the NFL, to the spot of the kick; in high school, to the 20-yard line if the ball enters the end zone, or otherwise where the ball becomes dead after the kick) or to the 20-yard line if that is further from the goal line, and possession is given to the other team. If the ball does not go out of bounds, the other team may catch the kicked ball and attempt to advance it, but this is usually not advantageous. One official is positioned under each goalpost; if either one rules the field goal no good, then the field goal is unsuccessful.

A successful field goal is signaled by an official extending both arms vertically above the head. A team that successfully kicks a field goal kicks off to the opposing team on the next play.

Touchdown

A touchdown is achieved when a player has legal possession of the ball and the ball crosses an imaginary vertical plane above the opposing team's goal line. After a touchdown, the scoring team is awarded a try. A successful touchdown is signaled by an official extending both arms vertically above the head.

Try for extra point

A try is more frequently called an extra-point attempt or a PAT (abbreviation of "Point After Touchdown"). Either one or two additional points may be scored during the try. The ball is spotted at the 2 yard line (NFL) or 3 yard line (college/high school), and the team is given one play to earn points:

— The offensive team may attempt to kick the ball through the goalposts, in the same manner that a field goal is kicked. This option is almost always chosen, because a two point conversion attempt is much riskier. If successful the team is awarded one point, referred to as an extra point. Because the extra point is almost always successful, sportscasters will refer to a team up by seven (not six) points as being "up by a touchdown".

— The offensive team may attempt to advance the ball via run or pass into the end zone, much like a touchdown on the extra-point attempt, except that it receives two points. This is called a two-point conversion. The success rate for two-point conversions is less than 40 percent in the NFL and college, making the two-point conversion attempt a risky tactic; thus it is usually attempted only when two points will help the team but one point will not. For example, suppose that it is late in the game with a score of 21-10 and the losing team scores a touchdown, making the score 21-16. The scoring team will usually attempt the two-point conversion, because if successful, a three-point deficit later could be matched with one field goal; failure to convert would result in a five-point deficit that would not be surmounted without another touchdown-a situation no worse than the four-point deficit achieved with a kicked extra point.

— Under college rules, if the defensive team advances the ball the length of the field into the other end zone on the try, for example by an interception or a fumble recovery, it receives two points. This is officially recorded as a touchdown scored by the defense. The NCAA adopted this rule in 1990. This scenario cannot occur under NFL or National Federation of State High School Associations rules; the ball is dead and the extra-point attempt is over immediately when the defense gains possession.

— In the extremely rare event that the offensive team scores a safety on the try, it receives one point. In college football, this can occur when, for example, the defense gains control of the ball and attempts to advance it, then fumbles it out of bounds in its own end zone. In the NFL, since the try ends once the defense gains possession, a safety can only be scored if a defensive player bats a loose (fumbled) ball out of bounds in the end zone.

— The officials' signal for a successful try, whether an extra point or a two point conversion, is the same as for a touchdown. After the try, the team that scored the touchdown kicks off to the opposing team.

Safety

The uncommon safety is scored if a player causes the ball to become dead in his own end zone; two points are awarded to the opposing (usually defending) team. This can happen if a player is either downed or goes out of bounds in the end zone while carrying the ball, or if he fumbles the ball, and it goes out of bounds in the end zone. A safety is also awarded to the defensive team if the offensive team commits a penalty which is enforced in its own end zone.

A safety is not awarded if a player intercepts a pass or receives a kick in his own end zone and is downed there. This situation, in which the opponent caused the ball to enter the end zone, is called a touchback; no points are scored, and the team that gained possession of the ball is awarded possession at its own 20 yard line. If the interception or reception occurs outside the end zone, and the player is carried into the end zone by momentum, the ball is placed at the spot of the catch and no safety is awarded.

A safety is signaled by a referee holding both palms together above the head, fingertips pointing upwards. After a safety, the team that conceded the safety kicks a free kick (a punt must be used in the NFL; a place kick or a drop kick is permissible in amateur) from its 20 yard line.

Fair catch kick

A free kick may be taken on the play immediately after any fair catch of a punt. In the NFL, if the receiving team elects to attempt this and time expired during the punt, the half is extended with an untimed down. The ball must be held on the ground by a member of the kicking team or may be drop kicked; a tee may not be used. This is both a field goal attempt and a free kick; if the ball is kicked between the goal posts, three points are scored for the kicking team. This is the only case where a free kick may score points. This method of scoring is extremely rare; it is only advantageous when as a team catches a very short punt with very little time left. Note that a team is unlikely to be punting with only a few seconds left in a half, and it is rarer still for punts to be caught near field goal range. The officials' signal for a successful fair catch kick is the same as for a field goal.

Officials

The game is officiated by a crew of three to seven officials. Every crew will consist of a referee, who is generally in charge of the game and watches action on the quarterback and in the offensive backfield; an umpire, who handles spotting the ball and watches action on the offensive line; and a head linesman, who supervises placement of the down box and line-to-gain chains. The crew may also consist of a line judge, back judge, field judge and side judge, in the order listed: i.e. a crew of five officials has a referee, umpire, head linesman, line judge and back judge.

Officials are selected by the teams in advance or appointed by the governing league. Note that unlike some other sports, no football officials-not even at the NFL level-are full-time employees of the league; they all officiate on a part-time basis.

During the game, the officials are assisted in the administration of the game by other persons, including: a clock operator to start and stop the game clock (and possibly also the play clock); a chain crew who hold the down indicator and the line-to-gain chains on the sideline; and ball boys, who provide footballs to officials between downs (e.g. a dry ball each down on a wet day). These individuals may be provided by the teams involved-it is not uncommon for a high school coach's son to act as ball boy for the team.

Free Kicks

A free kick is a special play which does not occur from scrimmage. The kicking team begins behind the ball, while the receiving team must remain at least 10 yards downfield before the ball is kicked.

A kickoff is a kind of free kick used to start each half, and also used to restart the game following a field goal or touchdown. At the beginning of a half, the kicking team is determined by coin toss. After a field goal or touchdown, the kicking team is the team which just scored. A kickoff must be either a place kick or a drop kick. A tee may be used, and the ball may be held by a member of the kicking team. The receiving team may recover and attempt to advance the ball at any time after the kick, but the kicking team may not touch the ball until it has traveled at least 10 yards or been touched by a member of the receiving team. The ball is usually kicked as deep as possible to the receiving team, in order to force the receivers to start far down the field, but sometimes a team will attempt to recover its own short kick, in a play known as an onside kick.

A free kick is also used to restart the game following a safety. The team that was trapped in its own end zone, therefore conceding two points to the other team, kicks the ball from its own 20-yard line. This can be a place kick (in the NFL, a tee cannot be used), drop kick or punt. In the NFL and high school, a free kick may be taken on the play immediately after a fair catch.

Penalties

Because football is a high-contact sport requiring a balance between offense and defense, many rules exist that regulate equality, safety, contact, and actions of players on each team. It is very difficult to always avoid violating these rules without giving up too much of an advantage. Thus, an elaborate system of penalties has been developed to "let the punishment fit the crime" and maintain a balance between following the rules and keeping a good flow of the game. Players are constantly looking for ways to find an advantage that stretches the limitations imposed by the rules. Also, the frequency and severity of penalties can make a large difference in the outcome of a game, so coaches are constantly looking for ways to minimize the number and severity of infractions committed by their players.

It is a common misconception that the term "penalty" is used to refer both to an infraction and the penal consequence of that infraction. A foul is a rule infraction for which a penalty is prescribed. Some of the more common penalties are listed below. In most cases when a penalty occurs, the offending team will be assessed a penalty of 5, 10 or 15 yards, depending on the infraction. Also, in most cases, if the penalty is committed while the ball is in play, the down will be replayed from the new position (for example, if the offense commits a penalty on a first-down play, the next play will still be first down, but the offense may have to go 15 yards, or farther, to achieve another first down.) But if a defensive penalty results in the ball advancing beyond the offense's first-down objective, the next play will be the first down of a new series. Some penalties (typically for more serious fouls), however, require a loss of down for the offense; and some defensive penalties may result in an automatic first down regardless of the ball position. In all cases (except for ejection of a player or, in rare cases, forfeiture of the game), the non-offending team is given the option of declining the penalty and letting the result of the play stand (although the Referee may exercise this option on their behalf when it is obvious), if they believe it to be more to their advantage. For some infractions by the defense, the penalty is applied in addition to the yardage gained on the play. Most personal fouls, which involve danger to another player, carry 15-yard penalties; in rare cases, they result in offending players being ejected from the game. In the NFL, if a defensive penalty occurs after time has expired at the end of a half, the half will be continued for a single, untimed play from scrimmage. Under college rules, any accepted penalty when time has expired at the end of any quarter results in an extension for one untimed down.

In the NFL, with three exceptions, no penalty may move the ball more than half the distance toward the penalized team's goal line. These exceptions are defensive pass interference, intentional grounding, and offensive holding - but in this last case the exception pertains only if the infraction occurs within the offensive team's own end zone, in which case an automatic safety is assessed (intentional grounding from the end zone also carries an automatic safety). Under college rules, the same half-the-distance principle applies, but any offensive fouls involving contact in their end zone (eg. holding, illegal blocking or personal fouls) result in a safety.

The neutral zone is the space defined by lines drawn through the ends of the ball parallel to the yard lines when the ball is spotted and ready for play. No player may legally have any part of his body in the neutral zone when the ball is snapped, with the exception of the center. Specific penalties most often fall into larger categories; the penalties here are listed as such.

Penalties against the offense

A penalty shall be called against the team on offense, or the team with possession of the ball, when...

— *Illegal procedure (5 yards)* - they commit any of a number of infractions in failing to adhere to the rules that govern action before the snap. Referee signal: two arms in front of chest with closed fists "rolling" around each other (same signal that basketball referees use to signal traveling). Illegal procedure includes, but is not limited to:

— *False start* - any player moves after they have gotten in their set position before the snap in a way that simulates the start of the play.

— *Illegal motion* - a player in motion is moving forward at the time of the snap. Referee signal: One arm in front of chest, palm open and down, with the elbow out to the side, moved away from chest.

— *Illegal shift* - a player is not in motion but is not set before the snap; more than one player is in motion at the snap; or after more than one player was moving (shifting), all eleven players have not been motionless for one second. Referee signal: two arms in front of chest, palms open and down, with the elbows out to the side, moved away from chest.

— *Illegal formation* - fewer than 7 players line up on the line of scrimmage (or more than 7 in the NFL); eligible receivers fail to line up as the leftmost and rightmost players on the line in the NFL; or when five properly numbered ineligible players fail to line up on the line.

— *Delay of game (5 yards)* - they fail to snap the ball before the play clock reaches zero. The 40-second play clock (25 seconds in amateur) starts running immediately when the previous play ends. If there is a timeout or other stoppage of play, a 25-second play clock starts from when the ball is spotted and declared ready for play. Referee signal: Upper arms extended out from the body, forearms bent toward the opposite arm, such that the arms lie on top of one another or that each arm touches the opposite shoulder.

— *Illegal touching* (5 yards) - Referee signal: one hand held up to shoulder, fingertips touching the shoulder; (NFL) two hands held up to shoulders, fingertips touching the shoulders.

— *Of a Forward Pass* - a forward pass first touches an ineligible receiver, that is, one of the five members of the interior offensive line. If the ball touches a defender first, any player may touch it, and defenders may freely make contact with receivers.

— *Of a Free Kick* - the ball, after the free kick, first touches a member of the kicking team prior to traveling 10 yards. This is most often seen on an

Onside Kick where a member of the kicking team prematurely comes in contat with the ball in an attempt to recover it. Like Illegal Touching of a Forward Pass, if a defender (member of the receiving team) first touches the ball, any player may touch it.

— *Ineligible receiver down field (5 yards)* - an ineligible receiver is past the line of scrimmage prior to a forward pass. Ineligible receivers must wait until the pass has been thrown and travels past the line of scrimmage to move past the line of scrimmage. This penalty is not imposed if the receiver is behind the line of scrimmage when he receives the pass. This exception has been added to accommodate the screen pass, where a receiver catches a ball behind the line of scrimmage behind a "screen" of offensive linemen.

— *Intentional grounding* - a forward pass is thrown intentionally away from eligible receivers so that the passer avoids being tackled for a loss.

— *NFL penalty:* 10 yards or spot of foul, whichever is farther from the original line of scrimmage, and loss of down. If the penalty occurs with less than a minute left in the 1st or 2nd half, a 10-second penalty is also enforced. If it occurs with 10 seconds or less left, the half automatically ends. The 10-second runoff does not apply if the penalized team uses any of the allotted time-outs in lieu of the runoff. The defense is not credited for a QB sack on intentional grounding penalties.

— *College penalty:* Spot of foul and loss of down; defense awarded a quarterback sack in some leagues.

— In both NFL and college, intentional grounding from the offensive team's own end zone constitutes an automatic safety unless the defense chooses to decline the penalty, which might only ever happen if the infraction had occurred on a fourth-down play. If the quarterback has moved outside of the area between his offensive tackles (the "pocket"), there is no penalty for grounding the ball if the quarterback throws the ball past the line of scrimmage. There is also no penalty for "spiking" the ball to stop the game clock, by throwing it directly into the ground. However, such an action must be executed immediately after the snap of the ball, before the quarterback demonstrates intent to make a forward pass.

— *High school penalty*: 5 yards from the spot of the foul and loss of down; defense credited with a quarterback sack.

— *Referee signal*: both hands held out flat, facing each other, in front of the referee, moving down together diagonally roughly from one shoulder to the opposite hip.

In the NFL, if the penalties above occur with less than a minute remaining in the half and the clock running, then a ten-second penalty is also assessed. The half automatically ends if the penalty occurs with 10 seconds or less remaining to be played with the clock running. The 10-second penalty does not apply if the clock is stopped when the ball is set for play and will not start until the ball is snapped, or if a team elects to use one of their time outs in lieu of the 10-second runoff. A team wanting to run the clock out in a close game cannot intentionally false start and use the 10-second rule to their advantage, because the run-off rule only applies to a team that is either losing or tied. Since the enforcement of the 10-second runoff, only one NFL game ended automatically due to a false start with less than 10 seconds remaining (in 2005 between Arizona and St. Louis). A pre-season game in 2006 between Houston and

Kansas City had the first half end automatically due to an intentional grounding penalty with less than 10 seconds left.

— *Offensive pass interference* - a player physically hinders a defender attempting to catch a pass, or pushes the defender in order to create separation to catch the pass. Referee signal: two arms in front of the body with palms out and fingers up, moved in a pushing motion out. NFL penalty: 10 yards from the previous line of scrimmage. Amateur penalty: 15 yards from the previous spot and loss of down.

— *Illegal forward pass (5 yards and loss of down)* - a forward pass is thrown from past the line of scrimmage, or when a second forward pass is thrown on the same play. Referee signal: One hand, flat, waved behind the small of the back. Defense credited with a quarterback sack in some college leagues.

— *Holding (10 yards)* - there is illegal use of the hands or arms while blocking, usually a grasp or a tackle of a defending player; an automatic safety is assessed if the spot of the infraction is within the offensive team's own end zone. Referee signal: one forearm vertically held in front of the body with a closed fist facing the referee's chest; the other hand grasping the first arm's wrist. The penalty is enforced from the previous spot, unless the infraction occurred beyond the line of scrimage or during a running play, in which the penalty is enforced from the spot of the foul. High school penalty: 10 yards from the spot of the foul.

Or, when a player on offense commits an illegal block, such as if...

— *Illegal block in the back (10 yards)* - a player makes any block from behind and above the waist. Referee signal: one forearm vertically held in front of the body with palm facing outward; the other hand grasping the first arm's wrist.

— *Clipping (15 yards)* - an illegal block from behind and below the waist. Referee signal: hand striking the back of the leg.

— *Blocking below the waist', also called a crackback block (15 yards)* - an illegal block, from any direction, below the waist by any offensive player not on the offensive line (e.g. wide receivers, quarterbacks and running backs), by any player after change of possession, by any player in high school with certain exceptions. Referee signal: both hands brought down, wrists turned inward, in a chopping motion across the front of the thighs.

— *Tripping (10 yards, 15 in high school)* - a player trips a defender near the ankles. Referee signal: one foot kicks the ankle of the other leg from behind.

Penalties against the defense

A penalty shall be called against the defensive team when...

— *Encroachment (5 yards)* - a defensive player crosses the line of scrimmage and makes contact with a player, or has an unabated path to the quarterback, before the snap. Unlike the offsides penalty, this penalty immediately halts play: the referees blow the whistle, the clock stops, and the offense does not run a play. In high school, any entry to the neutral zone by a defensive player is an encroachment penalty; the play cannot start with a player offsides. Referee signal: both hands placed on hips, with elbows pointing outwards.

— *Neutral Zone Infraction (5 yards)* - before the snap, a defensive player (most often a lineman), jumps into the neutral zone and "startles" an offensive player causing him to false start. Referee Signal: same as enroachment/offsides.

— *Delay of game (5 yards)* - a defensive player delays the game or hinders the offense in hurrying to make the next snap. This happens most often in the last two minutes of a half when the offense is trying to go down the field in a hurry. Referee signal: same as offensive delay of game.

— *Running into the kicker (5 yards)* - on a kicking play where the defense fails to touch ("block") the kicked ball, they run into the kicker/punter. If such an act occurs but is not flagrant, this penalty is assessed. If flagrant, the personal foul of roughing the kicker may be assessed instead.

— *Defensive pass interference* - a defensive player physically hinders an offensive player from catching a catchable forward pass that has not been touched by any other player. Referee signal: same as offensive pass interference - two arms in front of the body with palms out and fingers up, moved in a pushing motion out.

— *NFL*: An automatic first down and the ball is moved forward to the location of the interference - a devastating penalty if the play was a long pass. If the interference takes place in the end zone, the ball is placed on the one-yard line.

— *College*: An automatic first down. Penalty is 15 yards or the spot of the foul, whichever is closer to the previous line of scrimmage. The half-the-distance rule does not apply, unless the previous line of scrimmage was on or inside the 2-yard line. If the ball was snapped between the defensive team's 17-

yard and 2-yard lines, and the foul occurred inside the 2-yard line or in the end zone, the ball is placed on the 2-yard line.

— *High school:* 15 yards and an automatic first down; the half-the-distance rule always applies.

— At any level, if the receiver is interfered with behind the line of scrimmage, the defender cannot be charged with pass interference (although he may be guilty of a different penalty). This nuance in the rules almost never arises, but can conceivably occur on a screen pass. Pass interference is also rendered inapplicable if the ball was tipped by a player on either team prior to the contact being made, regardless of how slight or incidental the "tipping" was.

— *Illegal use of hands* (NFL: 5 yards and an automatic first down; college: 5 yards and an automatic first down unless the previous play was 1st and 10, making the next play 1st and 5; high school, 10 yards and the down repeated) - a player illegally uses his hands against a player on offense while attempting to ward off a block, cover a receiver, or tackle a ballcarrier. Referee signal: one forearm vertically held in front of the body with an open fist facing away from the referee's chest (closed first for a HS referee); the other hand grasping the first arm's wrist. There are several restrictions on how a defender may initiate contact, such as when...

— *Defensive holding* - a player grasps a player on offense while attempting to ward off a block or cover a receiver. Referee signal: one forearm vertically held in front of the body with a closed fist facing the referee's chest; the other hand grasping the first arm's wrist.

— *Illegal hands to the face* - a player pushes or hits as a player on offense in the head or helmet. Referee signal: One open fist in a pushing motion to the referee's chin.

— *Illegal contact* - a player makes significant contact with a receiver after the receiver has advanced five yards beyond the line of scrimmage, This rule was adopted in 1978, and its enactment is regarded as contributing to the dramatic increase in both passing yardage and scoring the NFL has witnessed since that time. Referee signal: One arm in front of the body with palm out and fingers up, moved in a pushing motion out.

— *Inadvertently contacting* the face mask (5 yards, automatic first down awarded in college only) - contacting the offensive player's face mask without grasping or twisting it, or a "touch and release" of the mask. Note: it is also a foul for an offensive player to touch an opponent's face mask, including when the runner stiff-arms a defensive player. Referee signal: One hand extended in front of the face, fist closed, and pulling down (simulating the grasping of the mask).

— *Personal Foul* (15 yards and a first down, except in high school, where the down is repeated) - a player commits a conduct- or safety-related infraction. If the officials decide that the action was particularly flagrant, the player in question can be ejected from the game. Referee signal: same as offensive personal foul, possibly followed by the appropriate signal for one of the following penalties:

— *Roughing the Passer* (15 yards and an automatic first down, all levels) - a defender continues an effort to tackle or "hit" a passer after the passer has already thrown a pass. The NFL standard is that a defender is allowed to take one step after the ball is thrown; a defender is penalized if he hits the passer having taken two or more steps after the ball leaves the passer's hand. Referee signal: arm moved in a passing motion.

— *Roughing the Kicker* (15 yards and an automatic first down, all levels) - a defender, having missed an attempt to block a kick, tackles the kicker or otherwise runs into the kicker in a way that might injure the kicker or his vulnerable extended kicking leg. This protection is also extended to the holder of a place kick. Referee signal: leg moved in a kicking motion.

— *Roughing the Snapper* (15 yards and an automatic first down, all levels) - on a punt or field goal attempt, the center is allowed to regain his balance and assume a protective position before he is contacted by the defense.

— *Intentionally grasping the face mask* - contact on an opponent's face mask which includes grasping or twisting the mask, and including using the mask to tackle an opponent.

— *Spearing* - tackling or otherwise contacting an opponent with one's helmet. (This technique is illegal because of the risk of neck injuries to the tackler.) Referee signal: arm extended, bent at the elbow, touching the side of his head with a closed fist.

Penalties against either team

A penalty shall be called against the offending team when.

— *Offsides (5 yards)* - any part of a player is in or past the neutral zone when the ball is snapped. Unlike offensive players, defensive players are not compelled to come to a set position before the snap, so if a defender jumps across the line but gets back to his side before the snap there is no penalty. In the case of an offsides penalty, play is not stopped, and the penalty is announced at the conclusion of the play. The non-offending team can thus decline the penalty and take the yardage gained on the play - unlike in the case of a false start penalty against the offense, whereupon the play is immediately stopped by the officials. Referee signal: both hands placed on hips, with elbows pointing outwards.

— *Substitution infraction (5 yards)* - the team has twelve or more players in the huddle or formation before a play or a player is attempting to leave the field as the ball is snapped. Referee signal: arm along the side of the body with the palm of the hand touching the opposite shoulder.

— *Illegal participation (15 yards)* - twelve players participate during the play, either because twelfth player is not detected before the snap or enters during the play. Illegal participation is also called when an offensive player goes out of bounds (unless forced out by contact by the defense) and returns during the play. Referee signal: two hands, palms down, touching the top of the head, with an elbow out to each side.

— *Sideline infraction (5 yards)* - when a coach or player on the sidelines is on the edge of the field during the snap. An official will usually issue a "sideline warning" once before issuing a penalty, and subsequent penalties will be unsportsmanlike conduct.

— *Personal fouls (15 yards, automatic first down in NFL and college if committed by the defense)* - a player commits a conduct- or safety-related infraction. This includes unnecessary roughness, such as hitting a ball carrier after he is already out of bounds, "piling on" a ball carrier who is already down, or violent contact with an opponent who is away from and out of the play. If the officials decide that the action was particularly flagrant, the player in question can be ejected from the game. Referee signal: Open fists held diagonally perpendicular and above the head, with the front edge of one hand striking the rear edge of the other hand near the thumb.

— *Unsportsmanlike conduct* - any person-usually a player, but occasionally a coach, and very rarely one or more spectators-acts or speaks in a manner deemed to be especially objectionable by the game officials, or by rule. Examples include throwing punches, deliberate physical contact with officials, verbal abuse of officials, and taunting, which, since 2004 in the NFL, has included any "prolonged and premeditated celebrations" by players (prior to that year these latter carried only a 5-yard penalty). Referee signal: both arms extended to the sides perpendicular to the body with open fists, palms down.

— *Violations of the equipment rules* - any player in the game without necessary safety equipment (mouthpiece, pads), without chin straps properly fastened, or in violation of certain clothing rules (e.g. sock requirements in college). HS penalty: 5 yards. College penalty: timeout charged against the offending player's team.

— *Palpably unfair act (as necessary)* - Called in the case of any illegal action that the officials deem has clearly and indisputably deprived a team of a score. For example, if a player or other person not legally in the game at the start of a given play comes onto the field to tackle a player apparently en route to a touchdown, the team that would have scored is awarded the touchdown. This can also conceivably be invoked in cases where the defense commits repeated intentional infractions very close to its own goal line.

Determination, Signaling and Assessment

During each play, any official may signal a penalty by tossing a bright yellow colored flag onto the field toward or at the spot of a foul. Multiple officials may flag the same play. If applicable, the same official can signal additional penalties on a given play by throwing a beanbag or his hat. When a flag is thrown, the referee, the official(s) who threw the flag(s) and other officials with a view of the play confer to come to a consensus on whether an infraction was actually committed, what it was, and who committed it. The final determination and assessment of the penalty is the sole responsibility of the referee.

The referee then makes initial visual body signals to the press box (and crowd) indicating what penalties were committed and the team that committed them, the latter shown by extending the arm toward that team's end zone. The referee then confers with the offended team's on-field captain to find out whether the offended team would rather decline the penalty and take the result of the play. However, there are certain scenarios where the referee may not have to confer with the team captain because the enforcement is entirely automatic (such as a false start penalty) or when the choice is fairly obvious (such as when the defense commits a foul during a play in which the offense scores a touchdown).

After any final conference, the referee then makes full visual signals describing the penalty in detail, which consists of: the penalty that was committed, the team that committed it, whether or not the opposing team chooses to decline it, and the resulting down or possession. In College Football, the NFL and other professional leagues, and in some high school games, the referee also announces the penalties over a wireless microphone to the crowd. In college and professional football, the referee will also give out the numbers of the players who committed the fouls.

Example: Suppose that, on a pass play in the NFL from the offense's 30 yard line, the safety, wearing number 26, commits defensive pass interference at the defense's 45 yard line. The official closest to the play, the side judge, throws his flag. After the pass falls incomplete and the play is whistled dead, the referee confers with the side judge and perhaps the umpire, who inform the referee of what they saw. The referee will likely then choose to assess the penalty.

The referee stands in the middle of the field, gives the pass interference signal and points to the defense's end zone. Since the penalty is very advantageous to the offense, the referee will likely assume that the penalty is not declined. After a short pause to confirm the penalty, the referee gives the full signal, displaying the body signals as he describes them: "Pass interference, number 26, defense. The ball will be placed at the spot of the foul. Automatic first down." The ball is moved to the defense's 45 yard line, and the next play begins.

Instant Replay

In the NFL, a number of rulings (but typically not penalties) can be reviewed by officials or challenged by coaches. If a coach wants to challenge a play, he must do so before the next play begins, and he does so by throwing a red flag similar to the officials' yellow flags. Coaches are allowed two challenges per game and may be granted a third if their first two are successful. The team loses a timeout if they lose the challenge. Plays inside the two-minute-warning cannot be challenged; any review of that play must be initiated by a replay official off-field. The referee performs the actual review via a video screen on the sideline. The referee will announce the result of instant replay reviews over his wireless microphone.

In college, coaches are allowed one challenge per game by first requesting a timeout. Otherwise, a replay official in the press box observes all plays. If he deems a ruling may be in error, he notifies the officials on the field to interrupt the game before the beginning of the next play. The replay official performs the review and relays the decision to the referee, who announces the result. Not every conference employs replay, which is optional.

High school rules do not provide for video review of any decisions by officials during the game. Further, the use of television or video tape for coaching purposes during the game is prohibited. If a coach feels a rule has been misinterpreted, he may call timeout and request a coach-referee conference to discuss the ruling with the referee, but no replay equipment will be consulted during the conference.

Players

Most football players have highly specialized roles. At the college and NFL levels, most play only offense or only defense.

Offense

— The offensive line (OL) consists of five players whose job is to protect the passer and clear the way for runners by blocking members of the defense. Except for the center, offensive linemen generally do not handle the ball.

— The quarterback (QB) receives the snap on most plays. He then hands or tosses it to a running back, throws it to a receiver or runs with it himself. The quarterback is the leader of the offense and calls the plays that are signaled to him from the sidelines.

— Running backs (RB) line up behind or beside the QB and specialize in running with the ball. They also block, catch passes and, on rare occasions, pass the ball to others. If a team has two running backs in the game, usually one will be a halfback (HB) or tailback (TB), who is more likely to run with the ball, and the other will usually be a fullback (FB), who is more likely to block.

— Wide receivers (WR) line up near the sidelines. They specialize in catching passes, though also block for running plays or downfield after another receiver makes a catch. A receiver lining up on the line of scrimmage is sometimes called a "split end" and a one lining up behind the line is sometimes called a "flanker".

— Tight ends (TE) line up outside the offensive line. They can either play like wide receivers (catch passes) or like offensive linemen (protect the QB or create spaces for runners).

At least seven players must line up on the line of scrimmage on every offensive play. The other players may line up anywhere behind the line. The exact number of running backs, wide receivers and tight ends may differ on any given play. For example, if the team needs only 1 yard, it may use three tight ends, two running backs and no wide receivers. On the other hand, if it needs 20 yards, it may replace all of its running backs and tight ends with wide receivers.

Defense

- — The defensive line consists of three to six players who line up immediately across from the offensive line. They try to tackle the running back if he has the ball before he can gain yardage or the quarterback before he can throw or pass the ball.
- — In most situations, at least three players line up as defensive backs, which are either cornerbacks or safeties. They cover the receivers and try to stop pass completions. They occasionally rush the quarterback.
- — The other players on the defense are known as linebackers. They line up between the defensive line and defensive backs and may either rush the quarterback or cover potential receivers.

Special Teams

The units of players who handle kicking plays are known as "special teams". Two important special-teams players are the "punter", who handles punts, and the "placekicker" or "kicker", who kicks off and attempts field goals and extra points.

Uniform Numbering

In the NFL, ranges of uniform numbers are reserved for certain positions:

- — 1-9: Quarterbacks, kickers and punters
- — 10-19: Quarterbacks, kickers, punters, and wide receivers
- — 20-49: Running backs and defensive backs
- — 50-59: Centers and linebackers
- — 60-79: Offensive and defensive linemen
- — 80-89: Wide receivers and tight ends
- — 90-99: Defensive linemen and linebackers

NCAA rules specify only that offensive linemen must have numbers in the 50-79 range, but the association "strongly recommends" that quarterbacks and running backs have numbers below 50 and wide receivers numbers above 79. This helps officials as it means that numbers 50 to 79 are ineligible receivers, or players that normally may not touch the ball.

Basic Strategy

Because the game stops after every down, giving teams a chance to call a new play, strategy plays a major role in football. Each team has a playbook of dozens to hundreds of plays. Ideally, each play is a scripted, strategically sound team-coordinated endeavor. Some plays are very safe; they are likely to get only a few yards. Other plays have the potential for long gains but at a greater risk of a loss of yardage or a turnover.

Generally speaking, rushing plays are less risky than passing plays. However, there are relatively safe passing plays and risky running plays. To deceive the other team, some passing plays are designed to resemble running plays and vice versa. There are many trick or gadget plays, such as when a team lines up as if it intends to punt and then tries to run or pass for a first down. Such high-risk plays are a great thrill to the fans when they work. However, they can spell disaster if the opposing team realizes the deception and acts accordingly.

The defense also plans plays in response to expectations of what the offense will do. For example, a "blitz" (using linebackers or defensive backs to charge the quarterback) is often attempted when the team on defense expects a pass. A blitz makes downfield passing more difficult but exposes the defense to big gains if the offensive line stems the rush.

Many hours of preparation and strategizing, including film review by both players and coaches, go into the days between football games. This, along with the demanding physicality of football, is why teams typically play at most one game per week.

Physicality

American football is a collision sport. To stop the offense from advancing the ball, the defense must tackle the player with the ball by knocking him down. As such, defensive players must use some form of physical contact to bring the ball-carrier to the ground, within certain rules and guidelines. Tacklers cannot kick, punch or trip the runner. They also cannot grab the face mask of the runner's helmet or lead into a tackle with their own helmet. Despite these and other rules regarding unnecessary roughness, most other forms of tackling are legal. Blockers and defenders trying to evade them also have wide leeway in trying to force their opponents out of the way. Quarterbacks are regularly hit by defenders coming on full speed from outside the quarterback's field of vision. This is commonly known as a blindside.

To compensate for this, players must wear special protective equipment, such as a padded plastic helmet, shoulder pads, hip pads and knee pads. These protective pads were introduced decades ago and have improved ever since to help minimize lasting injury to players. An unintended consequence of all the safety equipment has resulted in increasing levels of violence in the game. Players may now hurl themselves at one another at high speeds without a significant chance of injury. Unfortunately, the injuries that do result tend to be severe and often season or career-ending and sometimes fatal. In previous years with less padding, tackling more closely resembled tackles in Rugby football. Better helmets have allowed players to use their helmets as weapons. All this has caused the various leagues, especially the NFL, to implement a complicated series of penalties for various types of contact. Most recently, virtually any contact with the helmet of a defensive player on the quarterback, or any contact to the quarterback's head, is now a foul.

Despite protective equipment and rule changes to emphasize safety, injuries remain very common in football. It is increasingly rare, for example, for NFL quarterbacks or running backs (who take the most direct hits) to make it through an entire season without missing some time to injury. Additionally, twenty-eight football players, mostly high schoolers, died from injuries directly related to football from 2000-05, although many were related to dehydration or other examples of "non-physical" dangers, according to the National Center for Catastrophic Sport Injury Research. Concussions are common, with about 41,000 suffered every year among high school players according to the Brain Injury Association of Arizona.

Extra and optional equiptment such as neck rolls and knee pads help against injury as well, though they do not tend to be used by majority of players because of their lack of requirement.

The danger of football and the equipment required to reduce it make regulation football impractical for casual play. Flag football and touch football are less violent variants of the game popular among recreational players.

7

Australian Football

Australian rules football, also known as Australian football, Aussie rules, or simply "football" or "footy" is a code of football played with a prolate spheroid ball, on large oval shaped fields, with four posts at each end. No more than 18 players of each team are permitted to be on the field at any time, with four interchange players on the bench, and the primary aim of the game is to score by kicking the ball between the posts. After four 20 minute quarters the winner is the team who has the highest total score by the end of the match.

There are several different ways to advance the ball, including kicking and hand passing. When hand passing one hand must be used to hold the ball and the other fist to hit it - throwing the ball is not allowed. Players running with the ball must bounce or touch it on the ground every 15 metres. There is no offside rule and players can roam the field freely. Australian rules is a contact sport. Possession of the ball is in dispute at all times except when a free kick is paid. Players who hold on to the ball too long are penalised if they are tackled by an opposition player who is then rewarded, whilst players who catch a ball from a kick exceeding 15 metres (known as a mark) are awarded uncontested possession. The duration of play varies, but is longer than in any other code of football.

Frequent contests for possession including aerial marking or "speckies" and vigorous tackling with the hands, bumps and the fast movement of both players and the ball are the game's main attributes as a spectator sport.

The code originated in Melbourne, Australia in 1858, and was devised to keep cricketers fit during the winter months. The first laws of Australian football were published in 1859 by the Melbourne Football Club. The most prestigious professional competition is the Australian Football League (AFL), which culminates in the annual AFL Grand Final, the highest attended club championship event in the world. The league has governed the sport through the AFL Commission and the AFL Rules Committee, since it disbanded the Australian National Football Council in 1993.

Australian Rules Football in Australia

Australian rules football in Australia is a popular spectator and team sport which originated in Melbourne and has become an important part of Australian culture. The sport is played in every state and territory of Australia and is particularly popular in Victoria, South Australia, Northern Territory, Western Australia and Tasmania. In the states where it is not as popular as other winter sports, New South Wales and Queensland, it is rapidly growing.

Australia is currently the only nation in the world where Australian rules football is played professionally and while its participation is diverse, the sport is only played professionally by men. The sport has attracted more overall interest among Australians than any other winter sport for at least several years. A recent survey has suggested that the sport recently took over from swimming as the most popular sport in Australia.

It is particularly popular amongst indigenous Australian communities. Approximately 10% of all AFL players are of indigenous origin.

Football is the most highly attended spectator sport in Australia: government figures show that more than 2.5 million people (16.8% of the population) attended games in 1999. In 2005, a cumulative 6,283,788 people attended Australian Football League (AFL) premiership matches, a record for the competition. A further 307,181 attended NAB Cup pre-season matches and 117,552 attended Regional Challenge pre-season practice matches around the country.

As well as the AFL attendances, strong state competitions also drew crowds. Although crowds for local leagues have suffered in recent years, they continue to draw support, particularly for finals matches. The South Australian SANFL drew an attendance of 303,354 in 2005, the Western Australian WAFL drew an official attendance of 202,797 in 2004 and the Victorian VFL also drew strong crowds. As of 2005 the AFL is one of only five professional sports leagues in the world with an average attendance above thirty thousand.

According to OzTAM, in recent years, the AFL Grand Final has reached the top five programs across the five biggest cities in 2002, 2003, 2004, 2005 and 2006. Australian rules football has achieved a #1 rating in the sports category in both 2004 and 2005.

Some of the more popular regional leagues have the "match of the week" televised locally and free-to-air on ABC Television's state networks. In Victoria (ABV) and Tasmania (ABT) both show the VFL, in Western Australia (ABW) it is the WAFL, in South Australia (ABS) it is the SANFL and in the Northern Territory (ABD) it is both the NTFL and the SANFL (in the NTFL off-season). Some regional leagues also attract a national audience through free-to-air broadcasting on television networks such as ABC2, which includes the VFL, SANFL, WAFL, NTFL and Tiwi Islands Football League (Grand Final only). OzTAM began measuring these audiences in 2006.

Structure and Competitions

The most powerful organisation and competition within the game is the elite professional Australian Football League (AFL). The AFL is recognised by the Australian Sports Commission as being the National Sporting Organisation for Australian rules football. There are also seven state/territory-based organisations in Australia, most of which are either owned by or affiliated to the AFL. Most of these hold annual semi-professional club competitions while the others oversee more than one league. Local semi-professional or amateur organizations and competitions are affiliated to their state leagues.

Australian Clubs and Competitions

In 1877, the game's first league, the Victorian Football Association (VFA) was formed. Gradually the game - known at first as "Melbourne Rules", "Victorian Rules" or sometimes as "Australasian Rules" - began to spread from Victoria into other Australian colonies in the 1860s, beginning with Tasmania (1864), Queensland (1866) and South Australia (1873). The game began to be played in New South Wales in 1877, in Western Australia in 1881 and the Australian Capital Territory in 1911. By 1916, the game was first played in the Northern Territory, establishing a permanent presence in all Australian states and mainland territories. In Newcastle, New South Wales the Black Diamond league was founded by Victorian goldminers and the Black Diamond Challenge Cup remains Australia's oldest sporting trophy.

The precursors of the South Australian National Football League (SANFL) and the West Australian Football League (WAFL) were strong, separate competitions by the 1890s. However, factors such as interstate rivalry and the denial of access to grounds in Sydney caused the code to struggle in New South Wales and Queensland. A rift in the VFA led to the formation of the Victorian Football League (VFL), which commenced play in 1897 as an eight-team breakaway of the stronger clubs in the VFA competition. By 1925, the VFL consisted of 12 teams, and had become the most prominent league in the game.

The first intercolonial match had been played between Victoria and South Australia in 1879. For most of the 20th century, the absence of a national club competition - and the inability of players to compete internationally - meant that matches between state representative teams were regarded with great importance. Because VFL clubs increasingly recruited the best players in other states, Victoria dominated these games. The introduction of State of Origin rules were introduced in 1977 saw Western Australia and South Australia begin to win many of their games against Victoria.

In 1982, in a move which heralded big changes within the sport, one of the original VFL clubs, South Melbourne Football Club, relocated to the rugby league stronghold of Sydney and became known as the Sydney Swans. In the late 1980s, strong interstate interest in the VFL led to a more national competition; two more non-Victorian clubs, the West Coast Eagles and the Brisbane Bears began playing in 1987. The league changed its name to the Australian Football League (AFL) following the 1989 season. In 1991, it gained its first South Australian team, Adelaide. In the next five years, two more non-Victorian teams joined the league. The AFL, currently with 16 member clubs, is the sport's elite competition and the most powerful body in the world of Australian rules football.

Following the emergence of the Australian Football League, the SANFL, WAFL and other state leagues rapidly declined to a secondary status. Apart from these there are many semi-professional and amateur leagues around Australia, where they play a very important role in the community, and particularly so in rural areas. The VFA, still in existence a century after the original schism, merged with the former VFL reserves competition in 1998. The new entity adopted the VFL name and remained a primarily state based competition. State of origin games declined in importance, especially after an increasing number of withdrawals by AFL players, and Australian football State of Origin matches ceased in 1999. The second-tier state and territorial leagues still contest interstate matches.

Australian Rules Football Around the World

Australian rules football is a sport played in countries around the world. About 16,000 people play in structured competitions outside of Australia and at least 20 leagues that are recognised by the game's governing body, exist outside of Australia. In contrast, there are over 600,000 players in Australia where the game is at its strongest and overseas players make up less than 2% of the total players worldwide. Although semi-professional players have come from outside of Australia, no player to learn the game overseas has yet played a game in the Australian Football League.

The growth of Australian rules in the 19th Century and early 20th Century was rapid, but it went into rapid decline following World War I. After World War II, the sport experienced a small amount of growth in the Pacific region, particularly in Nauru, Papua New Guinea and New Zealand.

Australian rules football is emerging as an international sport much later than other forms of football such as soccer or rugby, but has grown substantially as an amateur sport in some countries since the 1980s. Initially the sport has grown with the Australian diaspora, aided by multiculturalism and assisted by exhibition matches and players who have converted to and from other football codes. In Papua New Guinea, New Zealand, South Africa and the United States there are many thousands of players and these countries. Canada, Japan, Denmark and Sweden have also shown strong potential in the sport amongst local players in the lead up to the 2008 Australian Football International Cup.

The AFL became the defacto governing body when it pushed for the closure of the International Australian Football Council in 2005.

Australian rules football is played professionally only by men in Australia and is major spectator sport only in Australia, with the exception of occasional exhibition games staged in other countries and carnival type events overseas. Almost as soon as the game was becoming established in Australia, it had spread to New Zealand and South Africa, initially due to the Otago Gold Rush and Witwatersrand Gold Rush. The game was further fuelled in South Africa by Australian soldiers in the Boer War.

There were reports of early competitions in England, Scotland and also Japan, started by expatriate Australians and servicemen. In New Zealand, where proximity to Australia saw a formidable league, quickly grew to a formidable 115 clubs by the turn of the 19th Century. As the game spread, it became known as Australasian Football, with delegates from New Zealand added to the newly formed Australasian Football Council. In 1908, New Zealand defeated both New South Wales and Queensland at the Jubilee Australasian Football Carnival, an event held to celebrate 50 years of Australian Football.

World War I saw the game being played by Australian servicemen around the world, particularly in Egypt and in Europe in France, Belgium and England.

Following the war, the game went into a sharp decline outside of Australia, with all domestic competitions dying out. National teams and international competition in the sport were non-existent for three quarters of a 20th Century. The return of many Australian expatriates from overseas goldfields and tours of duty combined with Australia's low profile on the world stage offered few opportunities for the game to grow during this time.

With the withdrawal of its New Zealand delegates, the sport returned to the title of Australian Football, governed by the Australian Football Council. Concerned primarily with the growth of their own domestic competitions, the Australian leagues and governing bodies made little effort to develop or promote the game until the 1950s, and the council's role was mainly to oversee the growing importance of interstate test matches.

Nevertheless, the longest running fixture outside of Australia, the annual Oxford University versus Cambridge University match in England has been held since 1921 and has emerged into a fierce rivalry, and worthy of half-blue status at Oxford. Apart from this match, however the game was rarely played in England.

The only overseas place where the sport has been continuously played is the former Australian trustee mandate of Nauru, which began both senior and junior local competitions in the 1930s. The sport was also introduced Territory of New Guinea in 1944 and the Territory of Papua in 1948. World War II saw some servicemen play the game overseas, particularly in Asia in countries such as Malaysia and Indonesia and Africa in Egypt and Algeria. During the Vietnam War, matches were even played by servicemen against the local Vietnamese.

In the 1960s, Australian leagues began to show some interest in expansion of the game outside of Australia. 1963 saw the first Australian rules football exhibition matches played in the United States. Australian state leagues began occasionally promoting themselves in this way throughout the following decades.

In 1967, it was reported in the VFL Record's "Footy Facts" column that Australian football clubs existed in Johannesburg, Pretoria and Cape Town and that the VFL was optimistic about the future of the game in South Africa. Little is known of how or when these clubs had formed or what later became of them.

Since 1967 there have been many matches between Australian and Irish teams, under various sets of hybrid, compromise rules. In 1984, the first official representative matches of International rules football were played, and these were played annually each October until 2006.

By 1975, Papua New Guinea had gained peaceful independence and test matches began to be played against teams from Australia. The first ever full international match involving Australia was played in 1977 at under 17 level between Australia and Papua New Guinea in Adelaide, with Australia taking the honours. Since then, Australia have been peerless in the sport and seldom compete at international level.

Despite these small advancements to the international aspects of the game, progress overseas was rarely covered in the Australian media.

In the late 1980s, successful VFL exhibition matches attracted large crowds and spawned fledgeling local competitions in both Japan and Canada. The Australian media showed only a token interest in the matches in London and Japan involving VFL clubs. It was during this decade that the sport was first televised in North America and the United Kingdom.

The largest barriers to growth of Australian rules football internationally have traditionally been distance, field availability and player numbers. With a total of at least 36 player required for a game and a cricket sized pitch, this made it difficult for organisers in countries where space was a premium, enclosed grounds were not available and attracting participants would prove difficult. While these factors were not a problem in Papua New Guinea or New Zealand, they did pose large problems to leagues in Europe, Asia and America. The more inventive of organisers began to accept modified versions of the game, such as 9-a-side, often played on any available field, open space, parks, soccer or rugby fields. These approaches to the game were highly successful. In the late 1980s, as these factors became less of an obstacle, amateur leagues were established in Japan (1987), England, Denmark and Canada (1989). In the case of Japan and Canada, these were directly sparked by VFL exhibition matches.

In the 1990s, the Australian diaspora had spread and amateur competition has grown in countries such as Sweden (1993), Germany (1995), USA (1996), Argentina, Spain and Samoa (1997), South Africa (1998), as well as a number of solely expatriate teams, mainly based in South East Asia.

During this time, the VFL had expanded to become the AFL and in turn commanded a greater national and international audience. Word of the sport grew out of AFL exhibition matches, cult television following and

Internet communication. North American fans formed an organization, AFANA, specifically to work for improved media coverage of Australian football.

The traditionalists in the governing bodies of Australia (which became the AFL) were reluctant to sanction any games which were not played exactly according to the Laws of the Game, and the AFL initially did not recognise leagues which played the game on fields that did not closely match the proper dimensions or had less than 16 players per side.

Since the 1990s, these attitudes have changed somewhat and the AFL and other development bodies have directly contributed to the development the game overseas. The International Australian Football Council (IAFC) was formed after football first featured at the Arafura Games in 1995. Since 1998, the Barassi International Australian Football Youth Tournament, endorsed by the AFL as part of its International Policy, has hosted several junior teams from other countries. Since 2000, fledgeling competitions have been established in countries such as Ireland (2000), Tonga (2002), Scotland, France and China (2005).

Television and the Internet have since helped to increase the awareness of the game outside of Australia. Inspired by successful Arafura Games competitions, the inaugural Australian Football International Cup was held in Melbourne in 2002, an initiative of the IAFC and the AFL. The first International Cup also marked the beginnings of a very small media interest in the international aspects of the game in Australia, which was evidenced by poor attendances at the tournament.

In recent years, the game has grown particularly strongly also in Papua New Guinea and New Zealand where local player numbers are booming. In overall percentage terms their increases are high in comparison to the overall growth of the sport in Australia, however their total player numbers are at least 200 times less, making senior competition involving Australia at open level unlikely until at least 2020.

In 2005, after 8 years of growing domestic competition, the South African government declared Australian Rules Football the sport for "the new South Africa", injecting government funding into the sport. In the same year, the Australian Football League negotiated the voluntary dissolution of the IAFC to retain the status of world governing body of the sport. The AFL brought on its own international game development initiatives and funding and many leagues around the world formally affiliated with the AFL.

In 2006, Pakistan, Indonesia, Catalonia, Croatia, Norway, Bermuda and East Timor joined the list of playing nations with local players participating. On July 3, 2006 the AFL announced that it had formed an International Development Committee to support overseas leagues. The AFL hopes to develop the game in other countries to the point where Australian football is played at an international level by top-quality sides from around the world. The AFL plans to host the International Cup regularly every four years, beginning in 2008, the 150th anniversary of the code. Following the AFL's interest in the internationalisation of the game, coverage in the Australian media grew substantially.

On April 14, 2007, Australia's AIS Under 17 squad competed against the South African national Australian rules football team in the historic first international match between the two countries at North West Cricket Stadium in Potchefstroom, South Africa.

International Competition

The first truly international competitor in Australian rules was New Zealand. In 1908 the Jubilee Australasian Football Carnival was held to celebrate the 50th anniversary of Australian rules football. New Zealand (then representing a total of 115 clubs) defeated both New South Wales and Queensland in the carnival but lost to Victoria and Tasmania.

The Arafura Games, held in Darwin, Northern Territory, Australia (a competition for northern Australia, South East Asia and Pacific Islands) were the first International games to have Australian football as a competition sport, rather than a demonstration sport in 1995. Papua New Guinea won the Gold medal and retained it in subsequent games. Other teams that have competed at Australian Rules in the games include Japan, Nauru and a Northern Territory indigenous team. The International Australian football Council (IAFC) was formed after the 1995 Games.

Inspired by successful Arafura Games competitions, the inaugural Australian Football International Cup was held in Melbourne in 2002, an initiative of the newly formed IAFC. The 2002 cup was contested by 11 teams from around the world made up exclusively of non-Australians. Ireland won the 2002 cup, defeating Papua New Guinea in the final.

In the interim years, Japan and New Zealand played an annual game as a curtain raiser to an AFL game: the New Zealand national team were victorious by 100 points in 2003, and so in 2004, a club side from Auckland played the game, which Japan lost by two points. The amateur Australian Convicts also toured and played several matches against sides from developing nations.

The second Australian football International Cup was held in Melbourne in 2005, under the direction of the guidance and funding of the AFL with New Zealand defeating Papua New Guinea in the final, with third place going to the United States of America. The third Australian Football International Cup will be held in Melbourne in 2008. In 2006 Denmark, Sweden and Germany competed in a tri-nations series, which will be repeted annually.

Other international competitions that include Australian ex-patriates are also held, including the EU Cup, which was first held in 2005 in London, featuring 10 teams.

Rules of the Game

Both the ball and the field of play are oval in shape. No more than 18 players of each team are permitted to be on the field at any time. Up to four interchange (reserve) players may be swapped for those on the field at any time during the game. There is no offside rule nor are there set positions in the rules; unlike many other forms of football, players from both teams disperse across the whole field before the start of play. However, only four players from each team are allowed within the 50m centre square before every centre bounce, which occurs at the commencement of each quarter, and to restart the game after a goal is scored. There are also other rules pertaining to allowed player positions during set plays (i.e., after a mark or free kick) and during kick-ins following the scoring of a behind.

A game consists of four quarters. The length of the quarters can vary from 15 to 25 minutes in different leagues. In the AFL, quarters are 20 minutes, but the clock is stopped when the ball is out of play, meaning that an average quarter could last for 27 to 31 minutes. At the end of each quarter, teams change their scoring end.

Games are officiated by umpires. Unlike other forms of football, Australian football begins similarly to basketball. After the first siren, the umpire bounces the ball on the ground (or throws it into the air if the condition of the ground is poor), and the two ruckmen (typically the tallest man from each team), battle for the ball in the air on its way back down.

The ball can be propelled in any direction by way of a foot, clenched fist (called a handball or handpass) or open-hand tap (unlike rugby football there is no knock-on rule) but it cannot be thrown under any circumstances. Throwing is defined in the rules quite broadly but is essentially any open hand disposal that causes the ball to move upward in the air.

A player may run with the ball but it must be bounced or touched on the ground at least once every 15 metres. Opposition players may bump or tackle the player to obtain the ball and, when tackled, the player must dispose of the ball cleanly or risk being penalised for holding the ball. The ball carrier may only be tackled between the shoulders and knees. If the opposition player pushes a player in the back whilst performing a tackle, the opposition player will be penalised for a push in the back. If the opposition tackles the player with possession below the knees, it is ruled as a low tackle or a trip, and the team with possession of the football gets a free kick.

If a player takes possession of the ball that has traveled more than 15 metres from another player's kick, by way of a catch, it is claimed as a mark and that player may then have a free kick (meaning that the game stops while he prepares to kick from the point at which he marked). Alternatively, he may choose to "play on:" forfeiting the set shot in the hope of pressing an advantage for his team (rather than allowing the opposition to reposition while he prepares for the free kick). Once a player has chosen to play on, normal play resumes and the player who took the mark is again able to be tackled.

There are different styles of kicking depending on how the ball is held in the hand. The most common style of kicking seen in today's game, due principally to its superior accuracy, is the drop punt (the ball is dropped from the hands down, almost to the ground, to be kicked so that the ball rotates in a reverse end over end motion as it travels through the air). Other commonly used kicks are the torpedo punt (also known as the spiral or screw punt; the ball is held at an angle and kicked, which makes the ball spiral in the air, resulting in extra distance) and the checkside punt or "snap", used to curve the ball towards targets that are on an angle. Forms of kicking which have now disappeared from the game include the drop kick (similar to the drop punt except that the ball is allowed to make contact with the ground momentarily before being struck with the foot) and place kick (where the ball is first placed on the ground when shooting for goal, similar to the place kick used in rugby union).

Apart from free kicks or when the ball is in the possession of an umpire for a ball up or throw in, the ball is always in dispute and any player from either side can take possession of the ball.

Scoring

At each end of the field are four vertical posts. The middle two are the goal posts and the two on either side, which are shorter, are the behind posts, or point posts.

A goal is scored when the football is propelled through the goal posts at any height (including above the height of the posts) by way of a kick from the attacking team. It may fly through on the full or bounce through and must not be touched, on the way, by any player from either team. A goal cannot be scored from the foot of an opposition (defending) player.

A behind is scored when the ball passes between a goal post and a behind post at any height, or if the ball hits a goal post, or if an attacking player sends the ball between the goal posts by touching it with any part of the body other than a foot. A behind is also awarded to the attacking team if the ball touches any part of an opposition player, including his foot, before passing between the goal posts. When an opposition player deliberately scores a behind for the attacking team (generally as a last resort, due to the risk of their scoring a goal) this is termed a rushed behind.

If the ball hits one of the behind posts, the ball is considered out of bounds and no score is awarded.

A goal is worth 6 points whereas a behind is worth 1 point. The Goal Umpire signals a goal with two hands raised at elbow height, a behind with one hand, and then confirms the signal with the other goal umpire by waving flags above his head.

The team that has scored the most points at the end of play wins the game. If the scores are level on points at the end of play, then the game is a draw.

As an example, consider a match between St. Kilda and the Sydney Swans. St. Kilda's score of 15 goals and 11 behinds equates to 101 points. Sydney's score of eight goals and ten behinds equates to a 58 point tally. St. Kilda wins the match by a margin of 43 points.

Origins of the Game

Tom Wills is widely credited with devising Australian rules in Melbourne in 1858. A letter by Wills was published in Bell's Life in Victoria & Sporting Chronicle on 10 July 1858, calling for a "foot-ball club" with a "code of laws" to keep cricketers fit during winter. His letter attracted other football players, and an experimental match, played by Wills and others, at the Richmond

Paddock (later known as Yarra Park next to the MCG) on 31 July, 1858, was probably the first game of Australian football. Unfortunately however, few details of the match have survived.

On 7 August 1858, two significant events in the development of the game occurred. The Melbourne Football Club, one of the world's first football clubs in any code, was informally founded, and a famous match between Melbourne Grammar School and Scotch College began, umpired by Wills. A second day of play took place on 21 August and a third, and final, day on 4 September. The two schools have competed annually ever since.

The Melbourne Football Club rules of 1859 are the oldest surviving set of laws for Australian football. They were drawn up at the Parade Hotel, East Melbourne, on 17 May, by Wills, W. J. Hammersley, J. B. Thompson and Thomas Smith (some sources include H. C. A. Harrison). The influence of English public school and university football codes, while undetermined, was clearly substantial. All members of the committee had experience of English or Irish games. Tom Wills, it is claimed, wanted to introduce Rugby School rules but the other three men felt Rugby School's rough play and offside rules would not suit players older than schoolboys or the drier Australian conditions. They did look at the Rugby School Rules but also those of Eton, Winchester and Harrow.

Finally eleven simple Melbourne Football Club Rules were laid out, printed and, most significantly, widely publicised. As other Clubs began, including the Geelong Football Club, there were some rival rules which eventually gave way to an acceptance of the Melbourne Rules. The rules did not include the requirement to bounce the ball while running which was introduced in 1866.

It is also often said that Wills was partly inspired by the ball games of the local Aboriginal people in western Victoria. Marn Grook, a sport that used a ball made out of possum hide, featured jumping to catch the ball for the equivalent of a free kick. This appears to have resembled the high marking in Australian football. The original recorded size of the Aboriginal playing field varies with records, but most records state that the playing field was about 1.6 km (1 mile) long. There were no goal posts, but teams played until there was a single winner, sometimes the side with the player who had the most possessions or the side that kicked the ball the most and the furthest. Wills was raised in Victoria's western districts and is said to have played with local Aboriginal children on his father's property, Lexington, near Ararat.

While it is clear even to casual observers that Australian rules football is similar to Gaelic football, the exact relationship is unclear, as Gaelic football was not codified by the Gaelic Athletic Association (GAA) until 1887. Long before either code existed, traditional Irish football games, known collectively as caid, were being played. Historian B. W. O'Dwyer points out that Australian football has always been differentiated from rugby football by having no limitation on ball or player movement (that is, no offside rule). The need to bounce or toe-kick the ball while running, and tapping the ball with one hand rather than throwing it, are also elements of modern Gaelic football. O'Dwyer suggests that some of these elements may be attributed to the common influence of older Irish games.

International Rules Football

Since 1967 there have been many matches between Australian and Irish teams, under various sets of hybrid, compromise rules known as International rules football. In 1984, the first official representative matches of

International Rules were played, and these were played annually each October between the AFL and the Gaelic Athletic Association between 1998 and 2006 as part of the official International Rules Series which have attracted large crowds and media interest in both Ireland and Australia.

Australian Rules is a sport rich in tradition and Australian cultural references, especially surrounding the rituals of gameday for players, officials and supporters.

As part of their uniform, players wear shirts called guernseys, a word possibly derived from the Irish (Gaelic) word "geansaí" meaning "sweater". Guernseys are similar to basketball shirts, but of a more robust design, often referred to in Australia as "jumpers". In the early period of the game's development players often wore sleeveless lace-up tops which gradually disappeared between the 1960s and early 1980s. A few players choose to wear a long sleeved variation of the modern guernsey design. Players wore full length pants, before adopting shorts in the 1920s. Tight-fitting shorts were a notable fashion trend in most leagues in the 1980s and some players began to wear hamstring warmers. A brief experiment with lycra by the AFL in the State of Origin series was quickly abandoned for more traditional wear. Padding is rare, but some ruckmen wear shin pads and thigh pads and players with head injuries sometimes wear soft helmets. Long socks (football socks) are compulsory, and mouthguards are worn by most players. Boots with moulded cleats or studs for gripping the ground are worn (screw-ins have been banned from most leagues since the 1990s).

Traditionally, umpires have worn white. However, in the AFL, umpires now wear bright colours chosen not to clash with the guernseys of the competing teams. AFL goal umpires now wear t-shirts and caps, rather than the traditional white coat and broad brimmed hat which was similar to what was worn by many cricket umpires. Australian rules is often referred to as the people's game due to its ability to transcend class and racial boundaries, unify supporters and attract crowds.

Fans barrack for their team rather than support or root for (in Australia, 'root' is slang for sexual intercourse). The term barrack is believed to derive from early matches between soldiers stationed in army barracks near the MCG. One of the first things many Melburnians will ask when meeting someone new is which football team they 'barrack' or 'go' for.

Typical supporter wear includes the team scarf and sometimes beanie (particularly in cooler climates) in the colours of the team. Team guernseys are also worn by supporters. Team flags are sometimes flown by supporters, and official club cheersquads behind the goals will sometimes wave enormous coloured pompoms known as floggers after the umpire has signalled a goal.

Meat pies and beer are popular consumables (sometimes noted as a tradition) for supporters at Australian rules matches. At AFL matches mobile vendors walk around the ground selling such pies, yelling out the well-known call of "hot pies, cold drinks!"

At the end of the match, it is traditional for a pitch invasion to occur. Supporters run onto the field to celebrate the game and play games of kick-to-kick with their families. In many suburban and country games, this also happens during quarter and half-time breaks. In the AFL in recent years, this tradition has been more strictly controlled with security guards to ensure that players and officials can safely leave the ground. At the largest AFL grounds, this tradition has been banned completely, to protect the surface, much to the discontent of fans. Sometimes a mid-game pitch invasion is expected for various highly anticipated landmark achievements (such as a player kicking a record number of goals). Australian rules football has attracted more overall interest among Australians than any other sport, according to the Sweeney Report.

It is the most popular form of football in the Northern Territory, South Australia, Tasmania, Victoria and Western Australia. It is less popular in New South Wales and Queensland, although there has traditionally been strong support for the code in regions within those states, such as parts of southern New South Wales including the Riverina and parts of Queensland such as Cairns and the Gold Coast. The AFL teams from Brisbane and Sydney have attracted a strong increase in crowds, television audiences participation when they both recently won premierships. Demographic and migration trends have affected all football codes in recent years, but most significantly Australian football in Queensland.

It is particularly popular amongst indigenous Australian communities. Indigenous Australians are well represented in professional AFL players: while only 2.4% of the population is of indigenous origin, 10% of AFL players identify themselves this way.

Australian rules is the national sport of Nauru and is popular in Papua New Guinea, which are both former Australian dependencies.

8

Gaelic Football

Gaelic Football, commonly referred to as "football", or "Gaelic" , is a form of football played mainly in Ireland. It, along with Hurling, is the most popular spectator sport in Ireland. Gaelic football is played by teams of 15 on a rectangular grass pitch with H-shaped goals at each end. The primary object is to score by kicking/striking the ball with your hand and getting it through the goals. The team with the highest score at the end of the match wins. Players advance the ball up the field with a combination of carrying, soloing, kicking, and hand-passing to their team-mates.

Gaelic football is one of four Gaelic Games run by the Gaelic Athletic Association, the largest and most popular organization in Ireland. It has strict rules on player amateurism and the pinnacle of the sport is the inter-county All-Ireland Football Final. The game is believed to have descended from ancient Irish football known as caid which dates back to 1537, although the modern game took shape in 1887.

Rules

Playing Field

The grass pitch is rectangular, stretching 130-145 metres long and 80-90 metres wide. There are H-shaped goalposts at each end with a net on the bottom section. The same pitch is used for hurling; the GAA, which organizes both sports, decided this to facilitate dual usage. Lines are marked at distances of 13m, 20m and 45m from each end-line. Shorter pitches and smaller goals are used by under-14s .

Duration

All Gaelic football matches last for 60 minutes, divided into two halves of thirty minutes, with the exception of senior inter-county games which last for 70 minutes (two halves of 35 minutes). Draws are decided by replays or by playing 20 minutes of extra time (two halves of 10 minutes).

Teams

Teams consist of fifteen players (a goalkeeper, two corner backs, a full back, three half backs, two mid fielders, three half forwards, two corner forwards and a full forward) plus up to fifteen substitutes, of which five may be used. Each player is numbered 1-15, starting with the goalkeeper, who must wear a different coloured jersey.

Positions

Like rugby and baseball, and unlike soccer, these have set positions which haven't changed in decades. In most cases, each player sticks firmly to his position, although players sometimes switch positions at the order of their coach, manager or captain.

Each team consists of one goalkeeper (who wears a different colour jersey), six backs, two mid fielders, and six forwards: fifteen players in all. Some under-age games are played 13-a-side (in which case the full back and full forward positions are removed) or 11-a-side (in which case the full back, centre back, centre forward and full forward positions are removed).

Goalkeeper

The role of goalkeeper who wears the number 1 jersey in Gaelic games is similar to other codes; to prevent the ball from entering the goal. The goalkeeper in Gaelic football and hurling also has the keep role of kicking the ball out to the outfield players, which known as fielding. A good goalkeeper most often has good agility and bravery as well as strength and height. In Gaelic football a keeper's shot stopping ability is of equal importance as their fielding. There is no limit to where on the field the goalkeeper can travel, although once they are outside of the 'penalty area,' they are subject to the same rules as all other players. A goalkeeper in men's football may touch the ball on the ground within the 'penalty area', and is the only player permitted to do so.

It is not permitted to physically challenge a goalkeeper while inside their own small parallelogram, but players may harass them into playing a bad pass, or block an attempted pass.

Right Corner Back

The role of the right Corner Back number who wears the number 2 jersey is to defend against opposing attackers, in particular the left corner forward. The right corner back will play most often from the end line to the 45 meter line.

Full Back

The role of full back who wears the number 3 jersey is one of the most important in Gaelic football or hurling. As well as defending against attackers, the Full Back is responsible for organizing the defense and is the key defender in front of goals, and is usually one of the physically strongest players on the team. The full back plays most often from the end line to the 45 meter line.

Left Corner Back

The role of the left Corner Back who wears the number 4 jersey is to defend against opposing attackers, in particular the right corner forward. The left corner back will play most often from the end line to the 45 meter line.

Right Half Back

The role of the right half back who wears the number 5 jersey is less defensive than that of the corner backs. The right half backs operate most often in between the 45 meter line and the midfield. The right half backs are expected to defend against the opposition's half forward line but also has a responsibility to make runs from the 45 meter line in order to advance the play to the half forward and full forward lines.

Center Half Back

The role of the centre half back who wears the number 6 jersey, is less defensive than that of the full back. The centre backs operates from the 45 meter line and forward to the midfield. The centre back will help win the breaking ball in the midfield and can be used as a 3rd midfielder. The centre half back generally marks the centre half forward.

Left Half Back

The role of the left half back who wears the number 7 jersey is less defensive than that of the corner backs. The left half backs operate most often in between the 45 metre line and the midfield. The left half backs are expected to defend against the opposition's half forward line but also has a responsibility to make runs from the 45 meter line in order to advance the play to the half forward and full forward lines.

Midfield

The role of the midfield who wears the number 8 or 9 jersey is to win kick outs / puck outs from either team's goalkeeper, and to act as the main link between the defending and attacking sections of the team. Midfield is often described as the most important role on the pitch.

If the opposing goalkeeper is kicking the ball to the middle of the field, the midfielder has the responsibility to retrieve the ball and therefore prevent the opposing team from taking advantage and bringing the ball forward. This then gives a new responsibility to the midfielder to get the ball moving forward to the half forward and full forward lines.

It is important for the midfield to have a good understanding of their goalkeeper. They must anticipate where their goalkeeper will place the ball and therefore take advantage and bring the ball forward.

Note that there is rarely a "left midfielder" and "right midfielder" - both play 'off' each other as a combined unit. Ciarán Whelan, with his immense high catching abilities, and Sean Cavanagh with his skill in creating attacks, are considered to be among the best Football mid fielders in Ireland at present. Paul Kelly of Tipperary and Jerry O'Connor of Cork were voted two of Ireland's best hurling midfielders in 2005.

Right Half Forward

The role of the right half forward who wears the number 10 jersey is to build up attacks and to feed the ball to the full forward line and also taking shots on goal or above the bar when opportunities present themselves. The half forwards will cover a lot of ground and utilizing speedy half forwards to run at defences is a common tactic. The right half forward operates from the midfield to the opposition's 45 meter line. The right half forward's main opposing player is the left half back.

Center Half Forward

The role of the centre forward (often called "centre half forward") who wears the number 11 jersey, is to build up attacks and feed the ball to the full forward line. The centre half forward is responsible for taking shots on goal and points when opportunities present themselves. The centre forwards will cover a lot of ground and utilizing speedy half forwards to run at defences is a common tactic. The centre forward also helps win breaking ball in the midfield, helping to win the possession in order to bring the ball forward. The centre half forward operates from the midfield to the opposition's 45 meter line.

Left Half Forward

The role of the left half forward who wears the number 12 jersey is to build up attacks and to feed the ball to the full forward line and also taking shots on goal or above the bar when opportunities present themselves. The half forwards will cover a lot of ground and utilizing speedy half forwards to run at defences is a common tactic. The left half forward operates from the midfield to the opposition's 45 meter line. The left half forwards main opposing player is the right half back.

Right Corner Forward

The role of the right corner forward who wears the number 13 jersey is to score points and goals. The full forward line is from the opposition's 45 meter line to their end line. The right corner forward is generally marked by the left corner back.

Full Forward

The role of the full forward who wears the number 14 jersey is to score goals in particular although points are usually the outcome of their attempts on goal. The full forward line operates from the opposition's 45 meter line to their end line. The full forward is generally marked by the full back.

Left Corner Forward

The role of the left corner forward who wears the number 15 jersey is to watch the full forwards breaks and to score as many points and goals as possible. The full forward line is from the opposition's 45 meter line to their end line. The left corner forward is generally marked by the right corner back.

THE BALL

The game is played with a round leather football, similar to a soccer ball, but heavier, and with horizontal stitching rather than the hexagon and pentagon panels often used on soccer balls, and similar in appearance to a standard volleyball. It may be kicked or hand passed. A hand pass is not a punch but rather a strike of the ball with the side of the closed fist, using the knuckle of the thumb.

The following are considered technical fouls ("fouling the ball"):

- Picking the ball directly off the ground
- Throwing the ball
- Going four steps without releasing, bouncing or soloing the ball. (Soloing involves kicking the ball into one's own hands)
- Bouncing the ball twice in a row
- Hand passing the ball over an opponent's head, then running around him to catch it
- Hand passing a goal (the ball may be punched into the goal from up in the air, however)
- Square ball, an often controversial rule: If, at the moment the ball enters the small rectangle, there is

already an attacking player inside the small rectangle, then a free out is awarded.

— Changing hands: Taking the ball from your right-hand to left or vice-versa.

Scoring

If the ball goes over the crossbar, a point is scored and a white flag is raised by an umpire. If the ball goes below the crossbar, a goal, worth three points, is scored, and a green flag is raised by an umpire. The goal is guarded by a goalkeeper. Scores are recorded in the format {goal total}-{point total}. For example, the 1991 All-Ireland semi-final finished: Meath 0-15 Roscommon 1-11. Thus, Meath won "fifteen points to one-eleven" (1-11 being worth 14 points).

Tackling

The level of tackling allowed is more robust than in association football (soccer), but less than rugby. The tackling rule has been criticised for being too vague.

Shoulder-charging and slapping the ball out of an opponent's hand is permitted, but the following are all fouls:

— using both hands to tackle

— pushing an opponent

— striking an opponent

— pulling an opponent's jersey

— blocking a shot with the foot

— sliding tackles

— tripping

— touching the goalkeeper when he is inside the small rectangle

— wrestling the ball from an opponent's hands

Restarting Play

— A match begins with the referee throwing the ball up between the four mid fielders.

— After an attacker has put the ball wide of the goals, the goalkeeper may take a kick out from the ground at the edge of the small square. All players must be beyond the 20m line.

— After an attacker has scored, the goalkeeper may take a kick out from the ground from the 20m line. All players must be beyond the 20m line and outside the semicircle.

— After a defender has put the ball wide of the goals, an attacker may take a "45" from the ground on the 45m line level with where the ball went wide.

— After a player has put the ball over the sideline, the other team may take a sideline kick at the point where the ball left the pitch. It may be kicked from the ground or the hands.

— After a player has committed a foul, the other team may take a free kick at the point where the foul was committed. It may be kicked from the ground or the hands.

— After a defender has committed a foul inside the large rectangle, the other team may take a penalty kick from the ground from the center of the 13m line. Only the goalkeeper may guard the goals.

— If many players are struggling for the ball and it is not clear who was fouled first, the referee may choose to throw the ball up between two opposing players.

Officials

A Gaelic football match is watched over by eight officials:

— The referee

— Two linesmen
— Sideline official/Standby linesman (inter-county games only)
— Four umpires (two at each end)

The referee is responsible for starting and stopping play, recording the score, awarding frees and booking and sending off players.

Linesmen are responsible for indicating the direction of line balls to the referee.

The fourth official is responsible for overseeing substitutions, and also indicating the amount of stoppage time (signalled to him by the referee) and the players substituted using an electronic board.

The umpires are responsible for judging the scoring. They indicate to the referee whether a shot was: wide (spread both arms), a 45m kick (raise one arm), a point (wave white flag), square ball (cross arms) or a goal (wave green flag).

All officials are also required to indicate to the referee, foul play or other misdemeanours he may have missed, but unfortunately this is a rare occurrence. The referee can over-rule any decision by a linesman or umpire. Dissatisfaction with officials is common in Gaelic football. Referees are often criticised for leniency and inconsistency, not seeing fouls, and playing an inordinate amount of stoppage time at the end of games (said to be hoping the losing team gets a draw). A common urban legend refers to a referee who was locked in the boot of a car after a Wicklow club game by unimpressed players.

History

The first mention of football in Ireland is found in 1308, where John McCrocan, a spectator at a football game at Newcastle, County Dublin was charged with accidentally stabbing a player named William Bernard. The Statute of Galway of 1527 allowed the playing of "foot balle" and archery but banned "'hokie' [sic] - the hurling of a little ball with sticks or staves" as well as other sports. However even "foot-ball" was banned by the severe Sunday Observance Act of 1695, which imposed a fine of one shilling (a substantial amount at the time) for those caught playing sports. It proved difficult, if not impossible for the authorities to enforce the Act and the earliest recorded inter-county match in Ireland was one between Louth and Meath, at Slane, in 1712.

By the early 19th century, various football games, referred to collectively as caid, were popular in Kerry , especially the Dingle Peninsula. Father W. Ferris described two forms of caid: the "field game" in which the object was to put the ball through arch-like goals, formed from the boughs of two trees, and; the epic "cross-country game" which lasted the whole of a Sunday (after mass) and was won by taking the ball across a parish boundary. "Wrestling", "holding" opposing players, and carrying the ball were all allowed.

During the 1860s and 1870s, Rugby and Association football started to become popular in Ireland. Trinity College, Dublin was an early stronghold of Rugby, and the rules of the English Football Association were codified in 1863 and distributed widely. By this time, according to Gaelic football historian Jack Mahon, even in the Irish countryside, caid had begun to give way to a "rough-and-tumble game" which even allowed tripping.

Irish forms of football were not formally arranged into an organised playing code by the Gaelic Athletic Association (GAA) until 1887. The GAA sought to promote traditional Irish sports, such as hurling and to reject "foreign" (particularly English) imports. The first Gaelic football rules, showing the influence of hurling and a desire to differentiate from association football - for example in their lack of an offside rule - were drawn up by Maurice Davin and published in the United Ireland magazine on February 7, 1887.

On Bloody Sunday in 1920, during the Anglo-Irish War, a football match at Croke Park was attacked by the British. 14 people were killed and 65 were injured.

Ladies' Gaelic football has become increasingly popular with women since the 1970s.

Gaelic Football vs. Australian Rules football

While it is clear even to casual observers that Gaelic football is similar to Australian rules football, the exact relationship is unclear, or even controversial. The Australian historian B. W. O'Dwyer suggests that there is circumstantial evidence that traditional Irish games influenced the founders of Australian rules. O'Dwyer argued that both Gaelic football and Australian rules are distinct from rugby in elements such as the lack of a limitation on ball or player movement - the absence of an offside rule. It has not been shown that other common elements of Gaelic and Australian rules, such as the need to bounce or solo (toe-kick) the ball while running and punching the ball (hand-passing) rather than throwing it were also elements of caid. For example, the requirement that players bounce the ball while running was not in the first Victorian rules (1859). There is no conclusive evidence to prove a direct influence of caid on Australian rules football.

Other unofficial accounts suggest that a relationship may have originated from the opposite direction: Archbishop Thomas Croke, one of the founders of the GAA, lived in New Zealand in the early 1870s (he was second Bishop of Auckland 1870 - 1874) and had the opportunity to witness Victorian Rules played there. Like Australian rules, the Irish football games of the 1880s allowed players to grab or push each other. If Croke was influenced by Australasian rules, the two games were soon developing and diverging in isolation from each other.

In 1967, following approaches from Australian rules football authorities, there was a series of games between an Irish representative team and an Australian team, under various sets of hybrid, compromise rules. In 1984, the first official representative matches of International rules football were played, and the Ireland international rules football team now plays the Australian team annually each October.

Since the 1980s, some Gaelic players, such as Jim Stynes and Tadhg Kennelly, have been recruited by professional Australian Football League (AFL) clubs and have had lengthy careers with them.

Leagues and Team Structure

All Gaelic sports are amateur; easing the strictness with which this is interpreted is advocated by the Gaelic Players Association. The basic unit of each game is organised at the club level, which is usually arranged on a parish basis, with various local clubs playing to win the County Championship at various levels:

— Senior: the better adult clubs

— Intermediate: junior champions compete in this the following season

— Junior: weaker adult clubs, from small communities

— Under-21

— Minor: under-18

— Under-age: all ages from under-17 down to under-9

On a national level, the team is organised on the old Irish county system, producing 34 teams representing the original 32 counties that cover the island of Ireland, plus teams representing the Irish diaspora in London and New York. Splitting Dublin into North and South due to its enormous population has been considered, but is unlikely to happen any time soon. There are also clubs in other parts of the USA, Britain, Asia, Australia, continental Europe and Canada.

Though Ireland was partitioned into two states in 1920, Gaelic sports (like most cultural organisations and all religions) continue to be organised on an all-island basis.

A team of 15 players plus substitutes is formed from the best players playing at club level.

Nearly all counties play against each other in a knock-out tournament known as the All Ireland Championship.

These modified knock-out games are organised on the four Irish provinces of Ulster, Munster, Lenister and Connacht.

In the past, the best team from each would play one of the others, at a stage known as the All-Ireland semi-finals, with the winning team from each game playing each other in the All-Ireland Final.

A recent re-organisation now provides a 'back door' method of qualifying, with knocked out teams getting another chance to win back into the competition.

County teams also compete in the National Football League, held every spring. The League is nowhere near as prestigious as the All-Ireland, but in recent years attendances have grown and interest, from the public and from players, has grown. This is due in part to the organisation of the league into the above format, the provision of the Division 2 final stages and the relatively new change of starting the league in February rather than

November. Live matches are shown on the Irish-language TV station TG4, with highlights shown on RTE2. In 2006, Kerry won the Division 1 title for the 18th time defeating Galway in the final. Louth defeated Donegal to win the Division 2 title.

The All Ireland Final

The final game of the inter-county series is the All Ireland Final which takes place on the fourth Sunday of September in Croke Park. Before 1999, the final was held on the third Sunday of the month, but this custom was changed due to an overloaded schedule of matches.

Over the four Sundays of September, All Ireland Finals in men's football, women's football, hurling and camogie take place in Croke Park, the national stadium of the GAA, with the men's decider regularly attracting crowds of over 80,000. Guests who attend include Uachtarán na hÉireann, An Taoiseach and leading dignitaries.

Two levels of the game are played at each All Ireland, the Senior team and the Minor team (consisting of younger players, under the age of 18, who have played their own Minor All-Ireland competition.)

The winning senior county football team receives the Sam Maguire cup. The most successful county in the history of Gaelic football is Kerry, with 34 All-Ireland wins, followed by Dublin, with 22 wins.

In 2006, Kerry took the Men's Senior Football Championship, defeating Mayo in the final, with Roscommon winning the Minor equivalent.

Ladies' Gaelic Football

Ladies' Gaelic Football is the most prominent amateur team sport for women in Ireland. It is also increasing in popularity in other countries around the world, often by members of the Irish diaspora

The game is very similar to the male form of Gaelic football, where two teams of 15 players kick or punch a round ball towards goals at either end of a grass pitch. There are two main competitions in this sport; the National League which is staged during the winter-spring months and is used as a warm-up to the All-Ireland Championship which is played during the summer. The All-Ireland Final is played on the last Sunday in September or the first Sunday in October in Croke Park, Dublin, where the winners receive the Brendan Martin Cup. The National League and Championship are organised by the Ladies' Gaelic Football Association.

Although most of the rules of the game are parallel to those for men's Gaelic football, there are some differences. The main ones are:

— Players may pick the ball directly from the ground

— All matches last 60 minutes: in the men's game, senior inter-county games last 70

— Goal kicks may be taken from the hand

— A countdown clock with siren is used if available: in the men's game, the referee decides the end of the game

— The game is less physical, with frees more likely to be given for what would be considered moderate tackles in the men's game

9

Street Football

The term street football encompasses a number of informal varieties of association football (soccer). These informal games do not necessarily utilise the requirements of a formal game of football, such as a large field, field markings, goal apparatus and corner flags, eleven players per team (with a minimum of seven per team), or match officials (referee and assistant referees).

Often the most basic of set-ups will involve just a ball with a wall or fence used as a goal, or items such as clothing being used for goalposts (hence the phrase "jumpers for goalposts"). The ease of playing these informal games means that they are popular all over the world.

Street football can be divided into three varieties: minor adaptations of the association football rules, games based on scoring goals and games which are not.

Rule Variations

Pick-up

This game is played similarly to a normal football game but with minimal rules and with any number of players, even two individuals playing against each other. The more complicated rules are often disregarded, mainly offside and the rule that keepers must not pick up a backpass. Tactics are much looser than in professional matches, with many teams effectively playing Total Football. In most cases the game is not timed, and the first team to score a set number of goals is the winner.

Goalkeeper Variations

Rush goalie

One player may take on the role of goalkeeper (i.e, become able to handle the ball), providing they are within, roughly, their own penalty area. This may be combined with other rules; the only prerequisites are that there are teams and two separate goals. This variation is commonly used to help mitigate a disadvantage, whether in numbers or skill. It's also known as "fly keeper", "goalie wag", "flie keeper", "any man saves" or simply "any man". Basically, when you are in a match and choose "rush goalie", it means that the goalie can come out but the 1st person on the same team must "rush" back to their goal to save the opposing team's shot.

A more restricted variant of rush goalie is that players must first announce that they are the keeper, for example by shouting "Keeps!" or "Switch keepers!" before they may handle the ball.

Small goals

Small goals is a descriptive name for a variation of football played informally: the goals are reduced to approximately 1-2 metres wide, and players are not permitted to touch the ball with their hands. No player has the role of goalkeeper, though a player may hang back and play a defensive role with their feet and other legal parts of the body. Small goals are used when playing Joga Bonito.

Stick goalie

Alternatively, especially when rush goalies are being used to ameliorate a difference in numbers, the side with more players may be forced to keep their goalkeeper in goal, known as stick goalie. Stick goalies are not allowed to leave their (albeit vaguely-defined) penalty area to participate in attacks, as opposed to the rush goalie who is effectively an outfield player who can handle the ball with their hands in the penalty area. While the terminology can be confusing if the rush goalie does not actually change, many times the rush goalie is actually of the sort described above.

Murder Ball/No rule/Death match/Foulie-footy/SoccerBrawl

There are no throw-ins, kick-offs, goal-kicks or corners. Fouls are allowed (as long as no one gets hurt), but hands aren't (apart from goalkeepers), if only to differentiate this game from rugby.

This game has come to dominate school playing fields and village greens when groups of young lads are challenged to a game of 'footy' by their footballing peers and see it quickly descend into a ball chasing blood bath.

However over recent years since the late 1990s, fair play has come into the spectrum, and people playing football in schools, colleges, university and with the friends acknowledge the following:

— No tackle from behind

— No shirt pulling

— No barging

— Play it where it lays rule (if there is a serious foul) either a drop ball is awarded or a free-kick.

— No handballing

— Not to go too far off the area of play

— If it goes past the goalkeepers line, it's a corner or goal kick
— Mini goal kicks

Games Based on Scoring Goals

Cubbies

This game requires at least three players and one goal. One of the players is designated as a goalkeeper. Players must try and score whilst stopping the other players from doing the same. Team play is optional, and any number of teams (or solo) players can take part.

Typical rules state that in the first round, one goal secures a player's progression to round two. Players that have scored wait (off the pitch) until all but one player has scored. In subsequent rounds, it is not uncommon for the number of goals required to match the round number, but usually only one goal is required.

Often, the place of the goalkeeper from round one is taken by the round's loser.

Many extra rules are often added to stop cheating such as no 'goal scrounging' (waiting by the goal to try and get your foot onto someone else's shot). In this variation, unlike most others, the keeper plays the role of referee, instead of the players deciding arbitrarily about fouls.

It is common for the 'No scoring inside the box' rule to be played. This is applied not only to make the rounds last longer, but also to help reinforce the no 'goal scrounging' rule. The rule dictates that no player can score from inside a 6 yard area of the goal (6 yard box if marked). In some cases, players will relax this rule and allow headers and even clean volleys to be scored from inside the box. This rule prevents players from simply running within a few feet of the goalkeeper and smashing it into the goal, making the game fairer for the keeper and for all outfield competitors.

The 2-Man(doubles)league consists of three teams of two or more teams. Two teams play at a time for five minutes with one of the other team players as the goalkeeper, only one net is used similar rules to the knock out games above. The aim of the game is to basically score as many as possible, sometimes the 6 yard area is used as a boundary which you're not allowed to shoot in. Each game won is 3 points, a draw being 1 point. Once a game is over, the other team(s) come on and rotate the fixtures after every game. The keepers will also rotate, one of the players from the team which isn't playing goes in net for the other two teams 5 minute match.

Each team plays each other twice, if two teams are level points at the end of it you sum up the goal difference to decide a winner.

Three-and-in

Score three goals and become the goalkeeper. A simple game, usually played for fun rather than to produce any winner.

Because successful players are faced with the (usually) undesirable task of being the goalkeeper, rules are often applied to ensure their stay in goal is not deliberately extended by unscrupulous players. This could mean a shot-clock being implemented (setting an 1-minute time limit for the next shot to occur).

Another rule to force players to shoot may be to change the goalkeeper every 5 goals or so, with the player having scored least going in goal. However, this can make the game resemble the above game more closely.

Three-in-three-out

Very similar to headers and volleys (below). It consists of three or four players, one of them acting as goalkeeper. The other (attacking) players must attempt to score three "valid" goals and win a run.

A goal is valid only if the scoring player received the ball from another player (as opposed to "from the ground"). A goal is "foul" whenever the player kicks a ball laying in the ground or kicks a ball "received from the ground". To put it simply, whenever the ball hits the ground, the next player to touch it is supposed to pass it to another attacker, so the latter can try a valid goal (usually by volley or header).

Whenever an attacking player scores a "foul" goal, he becomes the new goalkeeper, resetting the counter. The goalkeeper scores whenever the attacking players send the ball off-limits (i.e. missing the goal). When the goalkeeper scores the third point, the player responsible for the last offense becomes the goalkeeper and the counter is reset.

Boston Cage

This game requires playing with what type ot court is most common in the U.S., which is basketball courts. Teams gather at the court, or cage as it is referred to, and form teams of 4. There is 4 versus 4 until a player scores, by hitting the basketball pole with the ball. It cannot be behind the pole, or above where the poll curves outward to hold the basketball net. When a team scores, the losing teams rotates out for another team to play the winning team.

Heads and Volleys

This game in some forms requires only two players, however most often it needs at least three. In the game one player crosses the ball to another who must then either head or volley the ball into the goal which is defended by another player.

Dozens of different variations of the game exist, including the keeping of 'life tallies' (lives are lost by strikers if they miss, or by goalkeepers if they concede). An optional rule states that when the goalkeeper catches the ball they can then throw the ball to another player; if that player scores (a header or volley) then the original striker is put in goal.

In another variant a striker gains a point by scoring and the keeper loses a point; if the striker misses he loses 2 points and must become the goalkeeper. Other variants include the setting of shooting distances (e.g. shots are not allowed within 6 yards). In some more aggressive variants when a player loses all of their points each of the other players will take a turn to attempt to hit them from the penalty spot.

One version rules that if a shot goes wide or over, the player who had the last touch goes in goal. If a shot isn't volleyed or half-volleyed, again the shot-taker goes in goal. If an outfielder lets a shot go wide he/she goes in. If the keeper catches the ball before it bounces, or if it only bounces once, the player who touched the ball last goes in goal. If a player handballs it twice in one round (until another player goes in goal) they go in goal, however, if they handball it once or don't handball it before the round ends, they lose their handball count.

Also there is a variation of this game in which every time the player in goal concedes a goal he or she gains a letter towards a word (i.e HORSE) and when the word is spelled out the player has to face a wall whilst other players take shots at the loser's backside. This is called in the United Kingdom "Megasaurarse"

60 seconds

In this game, there is one goalkeeper and at least two outfield players. The goalkeeper will kick/throw the ball out, and begin counting to 60 at roughly one number a second. The outfield players must then cooperate to score a volley past the goalkeeper; should they do so, the count will be reset. If, however, the ball enters the goal without the kick being a volley, the goalkeeper catches a full volley, or the goalkeeper reaches 60, the last player to touch the ball becomes the goalkeeper. A variety of this game introduces levels, where initially only one goal must be scored, but every time the count is reset this goes up by one, so the players must score one, then two, then three, until they are unable to complete the allotted amount. There is considerable variety regarding what counts as a 'volley' or not - sometimes, it is permissible to lift the ball into the air and strike it into the ground yourself, whereas in other circumstances it is not counted as a full volley; also, whether volleying it in from a keeper's kick or throw is legal is a contentious point.

Points

This game is useful when there is a wide range in terms of age or ability amongst the players, and also requires a degree of sportsmanship between them. Players pass the ball around and shoot freely, but upon scoring, are awarded points by the goalkeeper according to the distance and/or skill level of the goal scored. This score is usually more generous towards younger players.

Points may also be awarded for a particularly good assist, or to the goalkeeper by the other players, if the keeper makes a good save. Points are usually awarded out of five; five typically being an outstanding acrobatic volley, one typically being a simple tap-in. Usually when a player reaches 20 points the goalkeeper is changed, either for the best or worst scoring player.

In this game, there is one player acting as goalkeeper and at least two outfield players. The aim of the game is to kick hard in the rear end of a bad goalkeeper which does not prevent to receive 25 points. In such case, each of the outfield players gains one free "rear end kick" to the goalkeeper. After that, the counting start again. The points are scored depending on the goal: normal kick: 5 points, head: 10 points, heel kick:15 points, overhead kick:20 points.

There is a clear demarcation of the goal post area. Inside this area the goalkeeper can move freely. Also, there is a demarcation of the field (often this is the big goalkeeper area). Of course, nobody wants to be goalkeeper. So, there is a set of rules to determine who will be:

— If a player touchs the ball more than one time, this player is the goalkeeper now (while the ball is in the air it can be touched many times)

— If a player shoot the ball outside of the scoring post

— If the goalkeeper throw the ball and he hits one of the players directly (like the game dodgeball)

Richard

The name comes from the Spanish verb rechazar ("to reject"). The players must reject the ball from their area (the limit is usually the middle line of the field) and score goals. After the ball is kicked across the middle, the player may only touch the ball up to three times (two times plus the shot). Richard is usually played with one or two players per side.

A goal gets one point, and two if the player shoots at once with no previous "touch" (and previously shouts that he/she will try to score double). A player may not stop a kick with the hand within the goal area. If that happens, or the player touches the ball in the opponent's area or toches the ball three times and it does not cross the middle line, a penalty kick is given to the opponent.

If one player kicks the ball hard enough so the other player can stop it with its chest (pechito, a Spanish diminutive for chest), the player can leave the area and touch the ball any number of times. The keeper must try to catch the ball (oustide the goal area or the rival's area) and throw it to the attacker's body.

Shooties

A game similar to "richard" for 2, 3 or 4 players, played within a confined 5-a-side pitch or walled space with goals. Each player may only occupy their half of the pitch, minus the 'D'goal area. No hands are used during play. One player 'kicks off' at the beginning of the game, after concedeing a goal or when the ball goes out of play. A kick off is taken with a 'dead ball' positioned within the player's own 'D', shots are direct. A player may block their opponents shot with any normally legal part of their body but only take one touch and only on shots which are, roughly, on target. After this one 'touch' to block a shot, or directly from a shot, the player who touched it can shoot at their opponent's goal. Games are generally played informally in 'sets', the first player or team to score ten goals winning.

When playing in teams the player who takes the first touch is the only person on that team who can then shoot, when the ball is touched by an opponent this is reset.

Tackle and Shoot

Like World Cup/Wembley, this game requires only one goal. The game can be played by as little as three people, with one goalkeeper, and two "attackers" both trying to win. Occasionally it may become two-a-side, often, rather than having a set match time, the "first to" rule is used, usually the amount of goals required to win is five. Rules are basically the same as football as we know it, except that out of play rules are different. If a player hits a shot wide, or over and the goalkeeper doesn't want to fetch it, he allows play to go on. The goalkeeper also doubles up as a referee. A rule that causes some arguments among players is the "deflections" rule. An example of a scenario when deflections are vital is this:

Two players, one A the other B, are playing tackle and shoot. The score is 4-4, and the next goal is the winner. Player A has worked amazingly hard, has ran and ran, but just can't get the final goal. Player B meanwhile, is leaning against the goalpost. Suddenly player A lifts a spectacular chip over the goalkeepers head, only for it to hit player B on the knee, and go in. Some "referees" say that player A should have the goal, as it was his shot, and was going in anyway, others say player B should have it, as it hit him last.

Pass and Shoot

Unlike tackle and shoot this is not competitive. Basically, any amount of players, pass it amongst themselves, using any amount of showboating and trickery, and score as many goals as possible. Occasionally players add rules such as one-touch, or all players must touch the ball before scoring, or they may see how many consecutive goals they can score.

Ten Shots

Quite like penalties, and is ideally played by two people. Both take it in turns to take shots at each other, and the winner, is the player who scores the most goals.

Four Nets

There are a number of nets, usually anywhere between

two and six. This is a game that is generally more fun with more people. Teams may consist of a few or many players, depending on how many players are taking part.

The objective is to score a set number of goals (usually three or five) into one of the opposing teams nets; when this happens, that team is out until the next round begins. The team which wins the most rounds are declared the overall winners. There is rarely a time limit, and the round will continue until one team remains.

There are a number of variable rules, such as Handball Nets, which means the Handball rule in football is reversed, and a foul is committed if a foot touches the ball.

The game can be played anywhere, with any sport that involves nets, and in almost any space. That is why it is one of the most popular forms of street football.

Gol Para Mi

This is usually a three player game. A goal is set up against a fence or wall using shirts, sticks or anything else as goal markers. The goal width is set by the players to make goals possible but not super easy. A player starts as goalie. Goalie can't use hands. Shots have to be at waist height or below. The non-goalies try to score a goal. When a player scores, they go into goal.

Games not Based on Scoring Goals

Keepie uppie

Keepie uppie is the art of juggling with a soccer/football using feet, knees, chest, shoulders, and head. It is similar to Kemari, a game formerly practised in the Japanese imperial court.

Panna

A game played 1 versus 1 in a small area. The idea of the game is to dribble the ball through the opponent's legs, which is called a Nutmeg. Once you have completed a nutmeg, the game is over. Note that you must retrieve the ball immediately after the ball has gone through the opponents legs. If the opponent gets the ball before you the game continues.

Nutmeg rush

This is played by any number of players, and can be done with anything that can be kicked. The aim is to score a nutmeg on an opposing player, and when this happens, they are open game for punches and kicks for ten seconds. This can be played on teams, with more than one ball, and a scoring system can also be attached.

Head tennis

Often played over a badminton or tennis net, this game uses the basic concept of tennis but only the head is used to play the football.

Slam

This a game loosely based on football and squash and is generally played by school children. The goal area is a hard surface such as a wall and the number of players can be variable. Each player takes it in turn striking the ball against the goal area. Each player must strike the ball from the where the ball ends up after the previous player's shot. A slight variation allows players to shoot .

Rules are very fluid and change dependent on available equipment, space or player numbers. In some versions, if a player misses, they are eliminated. In another version, any player can attempt to score at any time, except the person who scored the last goal. The winner in this version will be the first player to score a set number of goals, usually three. In variants with small participant numbers, players are given a number of 'lives' before they are eliminated.

Other names for Slam or variants include Wally (pronounced "Wall-E"), Bung, One-Touch, Dead Duck,Spot, Squash, and Wall Ball.

King of the Ring

This game is for a minimum of three players, but a number in excess of 15 is ideal.

Each player starts with a ball of their own in an area defined by low cones or a white line. The aim of the game is to be the last player in the ring - in control of their ball - after all other players have had the ball they started with kicked out of the marked area.

Attacker-defender

Often used as a training exercise, attacker-defender is a game for two people. One takes on the role of the attacker, the other takes on the role of the defender. The attacker begins in possession of the ball, with the defender a few metres away in a loose jockeying position. There is a target line a short distance (approximately 5-15 metres) away from the attacker, and the aim is to dribble the ball over the line without the defender gaining possession. If the attacker succeeds, it is a point to them and the roles are reversed, starting from scratch. If the defender tackles the ball from the attacker, then the roles are again reversed, but the positions are not reset.

10

Football Culture

Football culture is a descriptive term of the cultural aspects surrounding the game of association football. This article explores aspects surrounding the game itself, as well as that of the players, and society itself.

In many countries, football has ingrained itself into the national culture, and many parts of life revolve around it. Many countries have daily football newspapers, as well as football magazines. Football players, especially in the top levels of the game, have become role models and aspirational ideals for many people. The game itself has now become glamourised, with many children practising the game and aspiring to the wealth shown off by the top footballers.

Derbies

Derby matches, or matches between two neighbouring rival teams, are fiercely competitive and provide a spectacle in football, for the supporting fans as well as for interested onlookers. Sometimes there are underlying political and sectarian tensions. The term applies to matches between two local teams, that is in the same city or region. However it is sometimes erroneously used to refer to matches between big clubs from the same country - these can be found in the article **major football rivalries**. Examples of famous football derbies include:

— Luton Town v Watford - England
— Brighton & Hove Albion v Crystal Palace - England
— Tyne-Wear Derby - Newcastle United v Sunderland AFC - England
— El Clasico - Real Madrid v FC Barcelona - Spain
— Old Firm Derby - Celtic F.C. v Rangers F.C. - Glasgow, Scotland
— Merseyside derby - Everton F.C. v Liverpool F.C. - Liverpool, England
— Rome derby - Roma v Lazio - Italy
— Boca Juniors v River Plate - Buenos Aires, Argentina
— Colo Colo v Universidad de Chile - Santiago, Chile
— Ajax v PSV Eindhoven - Holland
— Klassieker - Feyenoord v Ajax
— Derby della Madonnina (Milan Derby) - A.C. Milan v Internazionale - Italy
— Derby della Mole (Turin Derby) - Juventus F.C. v Torino F.C. 1906 - Italy
— Fenerbahçe v Galatasaray - Istanbul, Turkey
— North London derby - Arsenal v Tottenham Hotspur - England
— Manchester derby - Manchester United v Manchester City, England
— America v Guadalajara - Mexico
— Tigres v Monterrey - Mexico

Food

In the United Kingdom, the attendance of football matches is also associated with consumption of what can be considered 'traditional football food'. Steak and kidney pies and meat and potato pies are a staple of food outlets in stadiums. (It must be noted that some people consider football stadiums the only place where people want to consume Bovril — and, bizarrely, London's exclusive Groucho Club.) Nowadays sales of food to fans raises a lot of income for clubs, and some clubs are now making an attempt to improve their service and diversify out of 'traditional' foods. In Brazil, sanduíche de calabresa (pepperoni sandwich) is a best-seller meal at the surrounding areas of stadiums after matches.

Match programmes

Match programmes are an integral part of football matches in the UK. The are sold inside and outside stadia before (and sometimes during) matches. In their most basic form, they provide basic information on the teams, players, and match officials. Larger clubs usually produce a multiple-page programme with a number of common features: comments from the manager and club captain, interviews with players, ex-players and backroom staff, information about ticketing arrangements for forthcoming matches, a detailed fixture list/review of the team's season so far, competitions, a page for the junior supporters' club, and/or a detailed feature on the opposition. Programmes from some matches are now collectible items, and can fetch a lot of money on auction.

"Fair Play"

"Fair Play" is the name of a FIFA programme which aims to increase sportsmanship as well as prevent discrimination in the game of football. This also involves programmes to reduce racism in the game. The programme extends to outside of football, in trying to support charities and other organisations which improve conditions around the world.

The principles of the Fair Play programme can be summarised as follows:

— Play fair
— Play to win but accept defeat with dignity
— Observe the Laws of the Game
— Respect opponents, team-mates, referees, officials and spectators
— Promote the interests of football
— Honour those who defend football's good reputation
— Reject corruption, drugs, racism, violence, gambling and other dangers to our sport
— Help others to resist corrupting pressures
— Denounce those who attempt to discredit our sport
— Use football to make a better world

Both FIFA and UEFA have awards which they hand out to individuals or groups of people who have promoted what they see as the 'spirit' of Fair Play, both within and outside of football. An example of this was the Italian player Paolo Di Canio who, while not given an award, was congratulated in many sections of the football world for a very generous display of "Fair Play". During a goal scoring opportunity while playing for West Ham United against Everton, the Everton goalkeeper picked up an injury, and Di Canio, instead of scoring what could have been the easiest goal of his career, caught the ball, thus stopping play and allowing the goalkeeper to receive treatment.

Football Chant

Football chants are chants generated by the crowd at matches to encourage the supporters' team, insult the opposition, or just make a noise. Teams tend to have their own 'anthems' which the crowds can sing; some songs are even shared between clubs. While some chants are used to mock opposition players (e.g. "Who ate all the pies?"), others are more aggressive and of a personal nature against a player on the field. Some chanting in the crowds can be more than insulting, and may even be racist or sectarian in nature; chants like these tend to have been banned from football stadiums.

Football Violence

The level of passion with which football teams are supported has from time to time caused problems, and clashes between fans can result in violence. Some violence occurs by people deliberately aiming to cause trouble, often after a match takes place, a phenomenon known as hooliganism. Other people engage in 'football firms', organized gangs that seek fights with firms supporting rival clubs. Both practices are said to have originated in England, and are sometimes known as the "English Disease",after the disorder caused by English fans travelling abroad to support either their club or national team in the 70's and 80's. However organised violence surrounding football has spread to other countries, most notably by the Ultras in Italy, the Torcidas Organizadas in Brazil and the Barras Bravas in Argentina.

Violence by fans has had varying degrees of seriousness, ranging from scuffles between fans to tragedies. There have been some incidents in fixtures abroad of fans being murdered: for example, two Leeds United supporters in Turkey in 2000. In recent years this aspect of the game seems to have passed its peak though it has by no means disappeared completely. Specialist police units and information-sharing between regional and international police forces has made it much harder for the hooligans to organize and participate in disorder. CCTV inside and outside stadiums and also at other anticpated "flash points" such as city centres and railway stations now makes it more likely that people involved in disorder may be identified later even if they are not arrested at the scene. However there are still disruptions surrounding football matches, an example being the UEFA Champions League matches which were played on March 12 and March 13, 2005.

Violence by fans has also affected players, but this is extremely rare. For example a message to Christian Vieri apparently by a Inter Milan fan threatened to burn down his restaurant, criticising his attitude towards the team. There is also the notorious incident where the Colombian international player Andrés Escobar was murdered shortly after returning home from the 1994 World Cup. This was reputedly for scoring the own goal which eliminated Colombia from the competition.

Accidents and disasters

There have been many accidents and disasters in the history of football. Some of these, such as the Hillsborough and Ibrox disasters, were due to problems with crowd control. The Heysel Stadium disaster was a combination of hooliganism and poor crowd control. The Bradford City Disaster occurred due to poor fire safety in the stadium. Lessons learned from these disasters have led to safer football stadia.

There have also been deaths on the pitch and dugouts:

On 5 September 1931, the Celtic F.C. goalkeeper John Thomson suffered a skull fracture when he collided with the Rangers F.C. player Sam English during an Old Firm match. He was fatally injured and died later that day.

On September 10 1985, Scotland national team manager Jock Stein died of a heart attack as his team scored the equaliser against Wales which virtually secured qualification for the 1986 FIFA World Cup finals. He was aged 62.

In 2003, Cameroon international player Marc-Vivien Foé collapsed during a match of the Confederations Cup against Colombia in 2003 and was pronounced dead later that day. His death was attributed to previously undiagnosed heart problems.

On 8 September 1990, York City's David Longhurst collapsed and died on the pitch during his team's match with Lincoln City. The game was abandoned. York paid tribute to the player later by naming a stand in his honour at their Bootham Crescent ground.

In 2004, the Hungarian international Miklós Fehér also died from a heart attack, while playing with Benfica against Vitoria Guimarães.

On 9 September 2006 Hinckley United player Matt Gadsby collapsed on the pitch during a Conference North game against Harrogate Town and Died. Medical tests have revealed he died from a heart condition known as Arrhythmogenic Right Ventricular Cardiomyopathy.

Several players have also been struck by lightning while playing during sudden storms.

Other disasters have occurred away from any stadia: most notably, the Superga air disaster of 1949 in which the entire Torino F.C. squad perished . The Munich air disaster, involving the 1958 Manchester United F.C team and the loss of the entire Zambia national football team in an air crash in 1993.

Stadia and Seating

The atmosphere at football matches is a major part of the whole experience for football supporters, and is also a major part of the "wow factor" that youngsters get when they go to their first football match. However, after the

Hillsborough Disaster, the British government of the time commissioned the Taylor Report which resulted in standing being banned from many places, to include every top league stadium. As a result, the atmosphere has suffered. Although it is clear that standing wasn't the sole cause of the tragedy, and that standing areas have been proved safe since, especially in Germany, the authorities in many countries still won't allow it. Groups like Stand Up Sit Down are campaigning for its return.

WOMEN AND FOOTBALL

Women have been playing football as long as the game has existed. Their numbers, as both football players and fans, increased with the lifting of bans on women playing football and attending matches. In Iran however women are still forbidden from attending matches, although many try to sneak into the stadiums. The first FIFA Women's World Cup was held in 1991, and has drawn worldwide television interest. Football matches now tend to have increased numbers of women supporters attending at the stadium itself, as well as watching the matches at home or in pubs or bars.

In the USA, the Women's United Soccer Association League was formed in 2001 in response to growing interest in women's football around that country. Unfortunately the league collapsed in 2003, but grassroots football was not affected in the country. The semi-professional W-League continues to operate with 38 teams Japan's women's league, the L. League is very well supported, and many other countries' women's football leagues are popular and growing.

Women's association football is the most prominent team sport for women in many countries, and one of the few women's team sports with professional leagues.

Women have been playing "football" for as long as the game has existed. Evidence shows that an ancient version of the game (Tsu Chu) was played by women during the Han Dynasty (25–220 CE). Two female figures are depicted in Han Dynasty (25–220 CE) frescoes, playing Tsu Chu. There are, however, a number of opinions about the accuracy of dates, the earliest estimates at 5000 BCE.

Association football, the modern game, also has documented early women's matches. In Europe, it is possible that 12th c. French women played football as part of that era's folk games. An annual competition in Mid-Lothian, Scotland during the 1790s is reported, too. In 1863, football governing bodies introduced standardized rules to prohibit violence on the pitch, making it more socially acceptable for women to play. The first women's match recorded by the Scottish Football Association took place in 1892 in Glasgow. In England, the first recorded game of football between women took place in 1895.

The most well documented early European team was founded by activist, Nettie Honeyball, in England, 1894. It was named the British Ladies Football Club. Nettie Honeyball is quoted, "I founded the association late last year, with the fixed resolve of proving to the world that women are not the 'ornamental and useless' creatures men have pictured. I must confess, my convictions on all matters where the sexes are so widely divided are all on the side of emancipation, and I look forward to the time when ladies may sit in Parliament and have a voice in the direction of affairs, especially those which concern them most." Honeyball and those like her paved the way for women's football. However, the women's game was frowned upon by the British football associations, and continued without their support. It has been suggested that exclusion of women was motivated by a perceived threat to the 'masculinity' of the game.

Women's football first became popular on a large scale during World War I, when employment of women in heavy industry spurred the growth of the game via company teams, much as it had done for men fifty years earlier. The most successful team of the era was Dick, Kerr's Ladies of Preston, England. Dick, Kerr's Ladies played in the first women's international matches in 1920. They played a team from Paris, France in April, and also made up most of the England team against Scottish ladies in 1920, winning 22-0. Dick, Kerr's Ladies returned to Scotland in 1921, for a second international with an audience of 6,000. They also toured Scotland afterwards, playing five matches for 70,000 people in the stands.

Despite being more popular than some men's football events (one match saw a 53,000 strong crowd), women's football in England and Scotland suffered a blow in 1921. The Football Association, in England, banned women from playing the game on Association members' pitches, on the grounds that the game (as played by women) was distasteful. A similar decree was made by Scottish football authorities. Some speculated that these decisions may have been driven by envy of the large crowds that women's matches attracted. The ban led to the formation of the English Ladies Football Association, and women's football matches were moved to rugby grounds and park football pitches not affiliated to the FA. The ban limited public exposure for women's football and slowed its growth, but did not stop it. Women's football continued to draw dedicated players and fans.

The English Women's FA was formed in 1969 (as a result of the increased interest generated by the 1966 World Cup), and the FA's ban on matches being played on members' grounds was finally lifted in 1971. In the same year UEFA recommended that the women's game should be taken under the control of the national associations in each country. In the 1970s, Italy became the first country with professional women's football players, albeit on a part-time basis. The first full-time professional team was the United States national squad, and in 1992, Japan was the first country to have a semi-professional women's football league.

At the beginning of the 21st century women's football, like men's football, has become professionalised and is growing in both popularity and participation. From the first known professional team in 1984, to the hundreds of thousands of tickets sold for the 1999 Women's World Cup, support of women's professional football (soccer) has increased around the globe. It is now the third most popular sport in the world

However, as in other sports, women have struggled for pay and opportunities equal to male football players'. Major league and international women's football enjoys far less television and media coverage than the men's equivalent. For instance the 2006 Algarve Cup, a significant international tournament, was televised very little in Europe (Eurosport did broadcast some games) and none at all in the USA (where the women's game arguably has the highest profile) and other regions. Another example is that FIFA's Women's web site links to information about the men's team. In spite of this, the popularity and participation in women's football is expected to continue growing.

One of the first modern pro women's teams was the US Women's Team, which played their first match in 1985. Japan has a sponsored league, called the L. League, which hosts friendlies, as well as football camps, striving to increase skills and level of play.

The Women's United Soccer Association in the United States, in the early 2000s, was the first true all-professional league for women anywhere in the world;

however, its ephemeral success was a setback for professionalism, and to date the top national leagues in the advanced countries, such as the Premier League National, the L. League, the W-League, Women's Bundesliga (Germany and Austria), Toppserien (Norway), Superliga Femenina (Spain), Women's National Soccer League (Australia), and others are either amateur or semi-professional.

For the Women's Olympic Football Tournament, given the general abandonment of amateur regulations in the Olympic Games in the 1990s, the national women's teams do not have restrictions due to professionalism or age, thus the tournament becomes a back-to-back re-World Cup with the best teams of the previous year's World Cup plus the hosts. However, England and other British Home Nations are not eligible to compete as separate entities because the International Olympic Committee does not recognize their FIFA status as separate nations, and it remains to be seen how the United Kingdom will be incorporated into the 2012 Olympic tournament, given that FIFA does not recognise the UK as a single sporting entity.

The growth in women's football has seen major competitions being launched at both national and international level.

In August 1917 a tournament was launched for female munition workers' teams in North-East England. Its official title was the "Tyne Wear & Tees Alfred Wood Munition Girls Cup," but it was popularly known as "The Munitionettes' Cup." The first winners of the trophy were Blyth Spartans, who defeated Bolckow, Vaughan 5-0 in a replayed final tie at Middlesbrough on 18th May 1918. The tournament ran for a second year in season 1918-19, the winners being the ladies of Palmer's shipyard in Jarrow, who defeated Christopher Brown's of Hartlepool 1-0 at St James's Park in Newcastle on 22nd March 1919.

Following the Football Association ban on women's teams in December 1921, the English Ladies' Football Association was formed. A silver cup was donated by the first president of the association, Len Bridgett, and this was competed for in the spring of 1922. 24 teams entered the competition, the winners being Stoke Ladies, who defeated Doncaster and Bentley Ladies 3-1 on 24th June 1922.

In 1937, Dick, Kerr's Ladies played Edinburgh Ladies in "The Championship of Great Britain and the World", but there was no formal international tournament until 1982 when the first UEFA European Competition For Representative Women's Teams was launched. The 1984 Finals was won by Sweden. This competition name was succeeded by the UEFA Women's Championship and today, is commonly referred to as the Women's Euro. Norway won, in the 1987 Finals. Since then, the UEFA Women's Championship has been dominated by Germany, which has won six of the seven subsequent competitions, including the 2005 Women's Euro.

The first Women's World Cup was held in China in 1991, and was won by the USA. The third Cup, held in the United States in 1999, drew worldwide television interest and a final in front of a record-setting 90,000+ Los Angeles crowd, where the home team won 5-4 on penalty kicks.

Prior to the FIFA's establishment of the Women's World Cup, a several unofficial tornaments took place, including the FIFA's Women's Invitation Tournament 1988, which was also hosted in China.

Besides the United States and Germany (which won the 2003 World Cup), the strongest women's teams have traditionally been Norway, China, and Sweden, with nations like Brazil and Canada emerging as powers.

In 2002, FIFA inaugurated a women's youth championship, officially called the FIFA U-19 Women's World Championship. The first event was hosted by Canada. The final was an all-CONCACAF affair, with the USA defeating the host Canadians 1-0 with an extra-time golden goal. The second event was held in Thailand in 2004 and won by Germany. The age limit was raised to 20, starting with the 2006 event held in Russia. Demonstrating the increasing global reach of the women's game, the winners of this event were North Korea.

The FIFA Women's World Cup is recognized as the most important International competition in women's football and is played amongst women's national football teams of the member states of FIFA, the sport's global governing body. Contested every four years, the first Women's World Cup tournament, named the Women's World Championship, was held in 1991, sixty-one years after the men's first FIFA World Cup tournament in 1930. The current format has sixteen teams competing every four years for the winner's trophy.

The participants qualify through the regional football confederations of Oceania (OFC), Europe (UEFA), North America, Central America and the Caribbean (CONCACAF), South America (CONMEBOL), Asia (AFC) and Africa (CAF). Of the first four tournaments held, the United States has won the championship twice, Norway once and Germany most recently in the 2003 tournament.

The tournament was originally the brainchild of the then FIFA president João Havelange. The inaugural tournament was hosted in China in 1991, with twelve teams sent to represent their countries. The 1995 FIFA Women's World Cup was held in Sweden with twelve teams. Over 660,000 spectators attended the 1999 FIFA

Women's World Cup in the United States, and nearly one billion viewers from seventy countries tuned in to watch sixteen countries vie for the title.

In the 1999 edition, one of the most famous moments of the tournament was American defender Brandi Chastain's victory celebration after scoring the Cup-winning penalty shot against China. She took off her jersey and waved it over her head (as men frequently do), showing her muscular torso and sports bra, as she celebrated. The 1999 final in the Rose Bowl in Pasadena, California had an attendance of 90,185, a world record for a women's sporting event.

The 1999 and 2003 Women's World Cups were both held in the United States; in 2003 China was supposed to host it but the tournament was moved because of SARS. As compensation, China retained its automatic qualification to the 2003 tournament as host nation and was automatically chosen to host the 2007 FIFA Women's World Cup. The host country for the 2011 FIFA Women's World Cup will be decided by vote in November 2007.

Since 1999, the finals have been contested by 16 teams. There are two stages: a group stage followed by a knockout stage. In the group stage, teams compete within four groups of four teams each. Each group plays a round-robin tournament, guaranteeing that every team will play at least three matches. The top two teams from each group advance to the knockout stage.

The knockout stage is a single-elimination tournament in which teams play each other in one-off matches, with extra time and penalty shootouts used to decide the winner if necessary. It begins with the quarter-finals, in which the winner of each group plays against the runner-up of another group. This is followed by the semi-finals, the third-place match (contested by the losing semi-finalists), and the final.

Since its conception in 1989, the Women's World Cup has continued to grow in popularity. FIFA estimates that there are currently forty million girls and women playing football around the world, and the number of women will equal the number of men by 2010. Planning for the 2007 Women's World Cup in China reflects the growth.

Drinking and disorder

In some countries football has been associated with alcohol consumption. This can be before, during and after the game, with drinking occurring inside the stadium (sometimes illicitly) as well as in pubs and bars outside. However, unwanted behaviour caused by drinking has led to the banning of the sale of alcohol to general supporters in stadia across the United Kingdom, although most English and Welsh sides continue to sell alcohol within general stadium areas, with only clubs in Scotland being subject to a blanket ban. Sales of alcohol still occur in executive lounges. Some teams and countries have supporters' clubs which have 'friendly' drinking reputations.

Pitch invasion

Pitch invasions are occasions when supporters move from the stands onto the football pitch for the express reason of disrupting a match. This has to be distinguished from times when, due to safety reasons, fans are let onto the pitch. Pitch invasions in football tend to be rare as clubs are punished heavily for letting any unauthorised persons on the pitch.

Mass pitch invasions tend to be rare, but famous examples can be found. One is the 1923 "White Horse" FA Cup final between Bolton and West Ham at Wembley.Due to the overwhelming numbers in the stadium the police had to bring order back to the stadium. Another example is the 1977 British Home Championship match between England and Scotland, again at Wembley. Here, after a Scottish 2-1 victory, the "Tartan Army" decided to invade the pitch and managed to break down the goalposts, as well as help themselves to some of Wembley's turf.

Solo invasions are more common although few in number. In some cases these people are streakers who try to invade the pitch while nude. Many supporters view this as harmless fun, although the security personnel at the club do not agree with this view. A more recent pitch invasion was at Euro 2004, where, in the final game between Portugal and Greece, Jimmy Jump ran onto the pitch to disrupt the game. Another famous 'invasion' was carried out by Karl Power, who managed to sneak into Manchester United's team photo before their Champions League game with Bayern Munich; his other stunts have involved the England national rugby union team and the British Grand Prix.

Sticker Albums

Usually collected by children, a sticker album is a book where a collector sticks in pictures of players from different teams in a certain league. The most widespread are those that have been produced by Panini worldwide. A Sticker Album can be compared to the USA's baseball cards.

Teams and players

From the beginnings of football clubs and players have contributed greatly to the culture of society. Teams have moved from amateur status to (in some cases) big commercial concerns. Players have also managed to increase their earnings massively during this change.

Football Clubs

Nowadays football has become big business for the privileged few. While most grassroot clubs and lower division league teams struggle to make ends meet, the big clubs can make a lot of money. Teams such as Manchester United and Real Madrid are considered amongst the richest in the world with a global support base. Chelsea has also undergone a transformation, buying up the services of many expensive football players, due to being bought by the billionaire Roman Abramovich.

The catalyst for this change was the arrival of satellite television. Satellite TV companies paid massive sums for the rights to cover football matches, and in turn have recouped this investment from the many fans who are unable to catch the game in person. This benefits the 'hardcore' and 'casual' fan as they have more choice of which game they want to watch.

While some clubs do well out of the increased money in football, other clubs can get into trouble trying to keep up. Leeds United attempted to do this by spending a lot of money, and were successful for a few seasons. However the debts became unmanageable, and the successful players were sold off, and the team were eventually relegated twice, first from the FA Premier League to the Football League Championship and later to League One.

Not all clubs do well out of television money. Clubs in lower leagues receive less money for matches and, if promoted to higher leagues, can have trouble matching the spending power of bigger clubs. This leaves them more likely to be relegated again.

Clubs from smaller countries also have problems with this issue. Due to their smaller population base they receive less money from television rights. This leaves them comparative paupers compared to clubs from the big countries, and can lead to debt problems if they try to match spending in trans-national competitions. Some clubs have managed to buck the trend by training players through their youth academies, as well as making wise investments. Examples of these clubs are FC Porto and Ajax Amsterdam, although it must be noted that when these teams become successful, as in Porto's case winning the 2003/04 Champions League, the team tends to get sold off due to financial pressures.

Corruption

Allegations of corruption, e.g. match fixing, in football have always been present. This level of corruption can vary from country to country, and can involve players, agents, and teams. The 2005-2006 football season saw many corruption scandals. This included the refereeing scandals of Robert Hoyzer in Germany, and Edilson Pereira de Carvalho of Brazil. This was followed by the 2006 Serie A scandal where five clubs so far have been found guilty of match fixing.

Football Players

Football players, especially in the top levels of the game, have become role models and aspirational ideals for many people. Josiah Cameron, of Sydney says that he sees numerous soccer stars as inspiration for his training, and how he plays the game. The game itself has now become glamourised, with many children practising the game and aspiring to the wealth shown off by the top footballers (it may be argued that for most footballers that this extravagant lifestyle is unrealistic). The top footballers also have "hangers-on", best compared to the groupies of rock stars. Such extravagance has recently been satirised in the UK TV show Footballers' Wives..

Bad Behaviour

While many footballers can be argued to be "good role models", there have been many headlines in the news regarding bad behaviour by footballers. Such is the influence of footballers, their activities tend to be reported widely in the media and also bring condemnation from the government of the countries of which they play.

One famous player was Diego Maradona. While he had exceptional skill and was voted FIFA's Player of the Century, he also suffered problems with drug abuse. He was also sent home from the 1994 FIFA World Cup for doping offences. His cocaine abuse has led to his medical problems in recent times.

There have been several incidents in UK of players being accused of violence and misconduct off the pitch. Although on many occasions, players have been found not guilty, such cases are very controversial. In 2001, two Leeds United players, Jonathan Woodgate and Lee Bowyer, appeared in court over the assault of a student outside a nightclub. Woodgate was found guilty of affray.] In 2002 three players, two from Chelsea and one from Wimbledon, appeared in court of charges of affray. All were acquitted.

In 2004, the Leicester City trio of Paul Dickov, Frank Sinclair and Keith Gillespie spent a week in jail after being accused of sexual assault while on a training break at the La Manga resort in Spain with their team. However, the case was dropped after forensic evidence showed the accusations to be baseless. Although the players accused were ultimately innocent, the scandal led to a media outcry about footballers and their behaviour, especially with regard to children who look up to them.

Wayne Rooney was also attacked in the media for alleged visits to prostitutes in 2004, a claim he later admitted was true. More recently, Adrian Mutu admitted cocaine use after failing a drugs test, and Graham Stack was charged with rape but cleared in 2005. Bowyer would again make headlines in 2005 when he and Newcastle teammate Kieron Dyer fought each other near the end of a Premiership match.

Ethnicity and Football

People of different races have sometimes not been accepted as players in European football. This is changing during the start of the 21st century due to societal change as well as campaigning on the part of the football authorities in different countries. UEFA and the European Union support the Football Against Racism in Europe (FARE) project which aims to stop racism. Many black players were not accepted initially into European football, even though the earliest black player was in 1881.

However in the 1970s onwards players were increasingly accepted leading to a situation where many club and national teams have players of varying ethnicities. However, full acceptance in the large footballing nations did not occur until the 1990s, and racism still exists at some levels: Samuel Eto'o, for example, was once racially insulted by some Real Zaragoza fans at a match against the FC Barcelona, and threatened to quit the game if they kept insulting him; the same happened to Messina defender Marc Zoro in a match against Inter Milan.

While smaller countries without a large ethnic population have been seen to have problems with racism, there have been recently notable incidents of racism in bigger leagues. There have also been problems with religious identity and football.

In some countries (England, Germany) there have been strong campaigns to remove racism and intolerance from football on the field and on the terraces. In other countries despite visible problems, little action has been taken (Spain, Italy).

Globalisation and Players

Globalisation has benefited current and former players, coaches, teams and others involved in football. For the best players it means their services can be offered to clubs in various different countries, and for whatever the pri they want. The top players can make salaries of millio in a year, plus whatever additional endorsements they receive.

Teams have also benefited from this by being able to find a wider support base outside their traditional local areas. They can also scout for talent from a wider area. However some European clubs have been accused of exploitation for doing this, as some African youngsters they have recruited for football teams have eventually been left with nothing after the team no longer requires their services.

Coaches are also becoming sought after expertise internationally. This extends to national team coaches, once being native to their country, being brought in from other countries. Examples include Brazilian legend Zico coaching Japan, Sven-Göran Eriksson, a Swede who coached England, as well as Berti Vogts, a German who until recently coached Scotland. Another German, Otto Rehhagel, is practically a national icon in Greece, especially after leading that country's national team to a shocking victory in Euro 2004, and shortly afterwards turning down an offer to coach the German national team to stay with Greece. Dutch coach Guus Hiddink has a similar iconic status in South Korea after coaching its national team to the semifinals of the 2002 World Cup—so much so that one of Korea's World Cup stadiums was renamed in his honor shortly after the competition.

Football in Modern Society

In many countries football has ingrained itself into the national culture, and many parts of life revolve around it. Many countries have daily football newspapers, as well as football magazines. The mood of regions and countries has been seen to be connected to football. Victory in a major tournament can bring happiness to the local community or country. Conversely defeat can lower spirits, and has been seen to be connected to mortality in the population. Withdrawal symptoms when the football season finished have also been reported.The economy can also be seen to be connected to major football tournaments, although the precise association is disputed.

The terms soccer mom and soccer dad (popularized in the USA) refer broadly to a demographic group of parents with school-age children playing football (soccer).

Arts, Literature & Film

The popularity of football has been reflected in the arts, books and films in many countries. Many books have been written dealing with the culture, such as violence, surrounding football, as well as detailed histories of events or rivalries. Many clubs have one or more fanzines, one example being TOOFIF.

Many consider that British football's image of a nasty working-class pursuit was changed into something far more respectable after Fever Pitch, a memoir (later adapted very loosely into a movie) by Nick Hornby about his life as an Arsenal fan, was published. The book also provided Hornby's big break. Films have been made ranging from the celebrated Bend It Like Beckham, to a more serious film, The Football Factory, based on the book by John King, dealing with hooliganism and it's relationship to socio-economic realities in Britain. In Germany, The Miracle of Bern revived the euphoria of the national team's victory in the 1954 FIFA World Cup and was a huge hit.One film that has a historical basis is Escape to Victory. This was based on the true World War II story where a Dynamo Kiev team, which defeated a German Luftwaffe team, was subsequently persecuted, and some team members executed. The story has also been recounted in the book Dynamo by Andy Dougan.

Football and Celebrities

Such is the popularity of football that some players become better known for their 'off-the-pitch' activities. The celebrity status is such that advertisers and sports goods manufacturers hire them to sponsor their products. The Brazilian footballer Pelé is such a player; he was so admired as a player during his time that he went on to become a UNICEF ambassador, as well as being a spokesman in advertisements for many different companies (most famously advertising Viagra). He also spent some time in politics in Brazil.

Former FIFA World Player of the Year, European Footballer of the Year, and African Footballer of the Year George Weah secured most votes in the first round of the 2005 Liberian presidential election, but was defeated in the run-off ballot.

Another (current) football celebrity is the English footballer David Beckham. While he is talented on the football pitch, he is also admired off it. He is a trend-setter in England, with his frequent hairstyle changes triggering copycat looks in the country. He is also married to the former Spice Girl Victoria Beckham, and his relationship difficulties were widely reported in the UK press in 2004 and 2005. Statues have been made of him, notably at a Buddhist temple as well as made out of chocolate.

Many other players have also become celebrities and are treated as heroes in the cities or countries that they have played for. Retired players, such as Gary Lineker, have also become celebrities in their own right by working on television or radio. Even non-footballers who are connected to football have become famous through their association alone. After the 2002 World Cup the head of the South Korean Football Association decided to run for president of the country.

Football as a Religion

It has been said that in some countries football has become the new religion. Many people tend to avoid their traditional places of worship, and are now regular attenders at football matches. Their devotion includes celebrating their footballing heroes, and it has been seen that people take time off to go and catch a glimpse of their idols. Other beliefs are also in common use throughout football. Many players are quite religious and can be seen to cross themselves before a game. In Africa, traditional belief rituals are used to help teams win important games. In Argentina an official religion around the football player Diego Maradona has been formed called "Iglesia Maradoniana".

11

FIFA

The Fédération Internationale de Football Association (FIFA) was founded in the rear of the headquarters of the Union Française de Sports Athlétiques at the rue Saint Honoré 229 in Paris on 21 May 1904. The foundation act was signed by the authorized representatives of the following Associations:

— France - Union des Sociétés Françaises de Sports Athlétiques USFSA

— Belgium - Union Belge des Sociétés de Sports UBSSA

— Denmark - Dansk Boldspil Union DBU

— Netherlands - Nederlandsche Voetbal Bond NVB

— Spain - Madrid Football Club

— Sweden - Svenska Bollspells Förbundet SBF

— Switzerland - Association Suisse de Football ASF

Representing France were: Robert Guérin and André Espir; Belgium: Louis Muhlinghaus and Max Kahn; Denmark: Ludvig Sylow; Netherlands: Carl Anton Wilhelm Hirschmann; Switzerland: Victor E. Schneider; the Madrid Football Club: André Espir; Sweden: Ludwig Sylow.

The first official international matches took place on the continent at the beginning of the century. The idea of founding an international federation began taking form. In general, one intended recognizing the leading role of the English who had already founded their Football Association in 1863. Thus, Carl Anton Wilhelm Hirschmann, secretary of the Netherlands Football Association, turned to the Football Association. Its Secretary did accept the proposal but until the Executive Committee of the Football Association, the international F. A. Board and the Associations of Scotland, Wales and Ireland had given their opinion about the matter, a great deal of time went past. Robert Guérin, Secretary of the Football Department of the Union Française des Sociétés de Sports Athlétiques and journalist with the "Matin" did not want to wait any longer. He greeted the Football Associations on the continent in writing and asked to study the possibility of founding an umbrella organisation. After an intensive exchange of correspondence, the first thoughts were made on the subject. Belgium faced France at the first official international match in Brussels on 1 May 1904. On that occasion, both Association secretaries Muhlinghaus and Guérin had a discussion. It was now definite that the Football Association, England under its President Lord Kinnaird would not be participating in the foundation of an international federation. So Robert Guérin took the opportunity and sent out invitations to the founding assembly. The services rendered by the founders were enormous. One began organising international football at a higher level.

The first FIFA Statutes were laid down. The following points were determined: the reciprocal and exclusive recognition of the National Associations represented and attending; clubs and players were forbidden to play simultaneously for different National Associations; recognition by the other Associations of a player's suspension announced by an Association and the playing of matches according to the Laws of the Game of the Football Association Ltd. Each National Association had to pay an annual fee of FF.50. Already in those days, one thought about staging a big competition and Article 9 stipulated that FIFA alone was entitled to take over the organisation of an international competition. It was decided that these regulations would only come into force as of 1 September 1904. Moreover, the first Statutes of FIFA were only of a provisional nature, in order to simplify the acceptance of additional members. The Deutscher Fussball-Bund (German F. A.) announced itself by cable on the foundation day still.

The first FIFA Congress held two days later on 23 May 1904 elected Robert Guérin as President. Victor E. Schneider (Switzerland) and Carl Anton Wilhelm Hirschmann (Netherlands) were made Vice-Presidents. Louis Muhlinghaus (Belgium) was appointed Secretary and Treasurer, with the assistance of Ludvig Sylow (Denmark). These pioneers were faced with an immense task because FIFA only existed on paper so to speak. One had to give it shape, create Associations as true national representations and get hold of new members. In the first place, the English had to be convinced that their membership to this newly created organisation was indispensable.

On 14 April 1905, the Executive Committee of the Football Association Ltd. recognized the National Associations affiliated to FIFA and joined. This was FIFA's first big success, thanks to Baron Edouard de Laveleye. With great personal efforts, the President of the Union Belge des Sociétés de Sports Athlétiques dissipated the last misgivings and doubts of the English. The Baron became the first honorary member of FIFA.

The second FIFA Congress took place in Paris from 10 to 12 June 1905. In the meantime, the Associations from Germany, Austria, Italy and Hungary had joined

FIFA; Scotland, Wales and Ireland would follow England's example. And one was already talking about an international competition to take place in 1906. It would consist of four groups and Switzerland would be in charge of organising the semi-finals and the Final. According to its meaning, one first thought of staging it with the best club teams. Moreover, the Swiss Vice President Victor Schneider had already donated a trophy.

The FIFA Executive Committee was elected for a further year in the same composition, but now the difficulties were accumulating. The first international competition was a failure. Various National Associations had other major worries. The French Football Association was split up internally. These difficulties were a heavy burden for the FIFA President who had set about his tasks with so much enthusiasm. Robert Guérin increasingly withdrew from the sports life and handed over the administration to his Vice-President Victor E. Schneider and André Espir, his personal assistant.

All the same, FIFA could now give a sign of its strength. When the "English Ramblers", an improvised English football club, wanted to play games on the continent without the authorization of the Football Association, FIFA forbade its members from playing against this team. The English who now had a good relationship with FIFA together with the 3 other British Associations, were particularly impressed by this strict and uncompromising procedure.

This was clearly revealed at the next Congress in Bern in 1906. Victor E. Schneider conducted negotiations in the absence of the FIFA President, Robert Guérin. The Englishman, Daniel Burley Woolfall was elected new President. He was a pragmatist and had gathered a great deal of experience on the administrative board of the Football Association. Under his guidance, English and continental football became more united. Moreover, he also launched an inexorable battle for uniformity in the Laws of the Game.

The idea of having a major international competition was still up in the air and so the Football Association assumed the responsibility for the administration and organisation of a tournament that took place within the context of the Olympic Games in London in 1908. Some problems arose in the organisation, which were still unsolved four years later in 1912, when the tournament took place in Stockholm. The new, virtually unknown sport was regarded suspiciously at the Olympics and was considered as a show and not a competition. In connection with the Olympic Games, the problem of professional players also arose - a thorny problem which would be pursued in decades to follow. England won both the 1908 and 1912 tournaments.

The Congress which, in accordance with the Statutes, was to be held in different cities on an annual basis, was always presided over by President Woolfall. The will to impose uniform football rules on an international level always figured at the top of the Agenda. This had a very positive effect, resulting in the basic rules of the organisation, which are still partly valid today and which allowed FIFA to create a solid base and develop clear guidelines in those days already.

Under the guidance of the English President, obvious progress had also been made in the administration. The first official FIFA bulletin was published. It was agreed to have French as the official language. The application of the Laws of the Game strictly established according to the English model became compulsory. A clear definition was made of international matches (selections and inter club) and outsiders were forbidden to organise matches for lucrative purposes.

FIFA only consisted of European Associations up until 1909. The first members from overseas joined in the following order: South Africa in 1909/1910, Argentina and Chile in 1912, USA in 1913. This was the start of FIFA's international activities. The long path towards full expansion had been sketched out.

The start of the first World War (1914) caused a major interruption. Who talked then about football and its mission to unite nations? And yet, all the international relations were not broken, even if they were only maintained on a small scale. International matches were still played, being organised on neutral territory. However, some members were faced with difficulties when having to cross frontiers and this prevented Congress being convened. The dream of having an international competition seemed to have evaporated forever. FIFA dozed on and President Daniel Burley Woolfall died in 1918.

That FIFA did not fade out completely, this was thanks to one man only: Carl Anton Wilhelm Hirschmann, who carried out his tasks as Honorary Secretary from his offices in Amsterdam and carefully kept the organisation alive. Within the scope of his limited possibilities, he maintained correspondence with his foreign colleagues. This way, he looked after the FIFA Secretariat on his own and at his expense. Hirschmann had an incredible capacity for work and was very unselfish. He dedicated his life to sports and particularly so to football. He served the Netherlands Football Association in various functions and also belonged to his national Olympic Committee. One of the founders himself, he took up contact with all the members at the end of the war, on the initiative of the President of the French Football Association, Jules Rimet. Hirschmann actually convened an assembly in Brussels in 1919. However, negotiations advanced tediously. After a long, bloody war, wounds had not yet healed. Many delegates, particularly the English, did not yet want to accept yesterday's foes.

So, a new meeting was held in Antwerp in 1920. A new administrative Board of FIFA was elected on a provisional basis. It was composed of the following: Jules Rimet as Chairman, the Dane, Louis Oestrup as Deputy Chairman and Carl Anton Wilhelm Hirschmann as Honorary Secretary.

The results of this election were then submitted to all affiliated Associations which unanimously gave their approval by mail. This was the last time that such a procedure was employed, as the next Statutes excluded voting by mail or by mandate.

Jules Rimet became 3rd President on 1 March 1921. FIFA became the life task of the then 48 year-old Frenchman. When he took over the world football federation, the latter which had been shaken by the I World War, counted 20 members. The British had left in unison and neither Brazil nor Uruguay were present. In the 33 years of his presidency, FIFA experienced an incredible upswing in spite of the II World War. One ought to talk about a "Jules Rimet Era" because he managed to reorganise FIFA and to materialize the dream of a World Cup. On passing on the reins of FIFA in 1954, when he opened his 5th World Cup in Switzerland, FIFA counted 85 members!

Right from the start, Jules Rimet was not unknown. He had already participated in the Congress in Christiania in 1914 as representative of the French Football Association. The following proposal was ratified on that occasion: " Under the condition that the Olympic Tournament take place in accordance with the Regulations of FIFA, the latter shall recognize this as a world football championship for amateurs." In order not

to lose every possibility of organising its own world championship, FIFA was ready to assume the responsibility for the organisation of the football tournament for the first time.

It was a great success right away and the results were surprising. 24 national teams entered. The English continued staying away from this tournament but the Americans were there and a team representing faraway Uruguay showed how football was played in South America, much to the delight of the public. Uruguay's results were astounding: 7:0 against Yugoslavia, 3:0 against USA, 5:1 against France, 2:1 against the Netherlands. 60,000 spectators followed the Final between Uruguay and Switzerland, which was won by the South Americans 3:0. Uruguay became the Olympic winners and were celebrated as world champions in Montevideo. South America's predominance was even more impressive at the Olympic Tournament in Amsterdam in 1928. Uruguay did not want to relinquish their victory on that occasion either. The opponents in the Final were Argentina.

This resonance at the Olympic Games intensified FIFA's wish for its own world championship. Questionnaires were sent to the affiliated associations, asking whether they agreed to the organisation of a world championship and under what conditions. A special Committee examined this problem. President Jules Rimet was the driving force in all sectors in the search for the means to materialize this dream. He was aided by the untiring Secretary of the French Football Association, Henri Delaunay.

Following a remarkable proposal of the Executive Committee, the FIFA Congress in Amsterdam on 28 May 1928 decided to stage a world championship organised by FIFA. Now, the organising country had to be chosen. Hungary, Italy, the Netherlands, Spain, Sweden and

Hungary submitted their candidatures. Right from the start, Uruguay was the favourite for important reasons: The country of the twofold Olympic winner (in 1924 and 1928) was celebrating its 100th anniversary of independence in 1930 at great expense.

Moreover, the Football Association was ready to take over all the costs as for example, the passage and accommodation of the participants. Any possible profit would be shared, while Uruguay would take over the deficit. These arguments were decisive. The FIFA Congress in Barcelona in 1929 assigned Uruguay as first organising country for the World Cup. The other candidates had withdrawn.

This decision did not only meet acclaim. Europe was plunged in the midst of an economic crisis. Participation in a World Cup did not only involve a long sea journey for the Europeans; the clubs would have to renounce their best, permanent players for two months. More and more associations broke their promise to participate, thereby seriously endangering the organisation of the World Cup.

Having nearly achieved his aim, President Jules Rimet was no longer impressed. Thanks to his personal effort, at least four European teams set off on the long journey: France, Belgium, Yugoslavia and Romania. The first World Cup was opened at the Centenary Stadium in Montevideo on 18 July 1930. A new epoch had begun for world football.

The World Cup in Montevideo became a remarkable success, both in a sporting and a financial sense. Of course, the organisers were disappointed since only four national teams from Europe participated. The anger in Montevideo was so intense that four years later, the World Champions - for the first and only time renounced defending their title.

The Congress convened in Budapest in 1930 and thanked Uruguay for staging the World Cup for the first time in difficult conditions. On the other hand, it regretted seeing only a minimum number of teams participating from Europe.

Another setback came in 1932. Before the Olympic Games in Los Angeles, differences of opinion could not be clarified on the international Olympic Committee regarding the amateur status of football players. So, FIFA decided not to organise an Olympic Football Tournament.

Sweden and Italy applied as candidate countries for the 2nd series of the World Cup at the 1932 Congress in Stockholm. The Executive Committee decided on Italy. Qualifying matches had to be played in order to arrive at the 16 finalists. Right from the start, the Cup system applied and so, the national teams from Brazil and Argentina already had to return home after their first defeat. Once again, the home team prevailed: Italy won the Final against Czechoslovakia in extra-time. For the first time ever, the World Cup Final was being transmitted on the radio.

Four years later, the "Father of the World-Cup" Jules Rimet saw his wish fulfilled, when the 3rd World Cup took place in France, his home country. Again, the tournament was plunged in shadows: Austria had disappeared from the scene and so Sweden did not have an opponent in the 1/8 final. Uruguay still did not want to participate and Argentina withdrew. This is why the national teams from Cuba and the Dutch East Indies came to France. This time, there was no home victory and Italy successfully defended their title. The World Cup should have taken place for the 4th time in 1942. However, the appointment of an organiser was renounced at the Congress in Paris in 1938. The 1942 World Cup never took place. One had to wait until 1 July

1946 for the next Congress which took place in Luxembourg. 34 Associations were represented at the Congress there. They presented President Jules Rimet who had been heading FIFA for a quarter of a century already, with a very beautiful Jubilee gift. From now on, the World Cup would be called the "Jules Rimet Cup". There was only one candidate for the next World Cup, to be staged in 1949 (and postponed to 1950 for time reasons). Brazil was chosen unanimously. At the same time, Switzerland was given the option for 1954.

1946 saw the return of the four British Associations to FIFA. This was again thanks to the diplomatic talent of Jules Rimet who found in Arthur Drewry and Sir Stanley Rous farsighted partners in the other party. Both would head FIFA in later years. Moreover, the event was celebrated later with a match between Great Britain and 'Rest of Europe XI' played at Hampden Park, Glasgow on 10 May 1947. Titled " Match of the Century" by the press, it was attended by a total of 135,000 spectators and receipts amounted to £35,000. As a sign of goodwill, this sum was placed at FIFA's disposal in order to help the latter get over financial difficulties brought on by the war years. The British won 6:1.

Brazil lost their 1st World Cup title in the Final against Uruguay. For the second time, the "Jules Rimet Cup" remained in Montevideo for four years.

Four years later, at the 5th World Cup in Switzerland, which was inaugurated by Jules Rimet in Lausanne, the 80 year-old President retired at the Congress in Bern. The delegates stood for one minute's ovation after his parting speech. He became the first Honorary President on that 21 June 1954. For the last time, the " Father of the World Cup" presented the captain of the victorious German team, Fritz Walter, with the "Jules Rimet Cup" and so departed from the top rank.

The Belgian, Rodolphe William Seeldrayers was the fourth President of FIFA. In his new function, he could celebrate the 50th Anniversary of FIFA, which now counted 85 members. After having assisted Jules Rimet as Vice-President for over 25 years, he died in October 1955. His successor was Arthur Drewry who was elected on 9 June 1956, but had already headed FIFA for over half a year on an interim basis. He chaired the Study Committee for the new FIFA Statutes and opened the 6th World Cup in Stockholm in 1958. This proceeded very positively and saw Brazil become the clear winners. Arthur Drewry died on 25 March 1961 at 70.

FIFA operations were controlled by the Swiss, Ernst B. Thommen until the Extraordinary Congress on 28 September 1961. As Chairman of the Organising Committee for the 1954,1958 and 1962 World Cups, he did a great deal for the world football federation.

Sir Stanley Rous was elected 6th President of FIFA. He was an excellent referee in his youth and was well acquainted with international football. During his term of office as President, England won the 1966 World Cup to his special joy. He was very popular throughout the world. Among the first steps taken by newly independent nations was their affiliation to FIFA. So, the number of members grew steadily. The TV transmission of the World Cup also considerably contributed towards the worldwide expansion. FIFA was rather conservative in those days and reserved in its decisions. Its means and possibilities were restricted. As a private institution, it received neither governmental subsidies nor funds from other sources. Funds strictly came from profits from the World Cup and this is how one had to live and work for four years. It hardly seemed possible to accomplish more without taking risks. Thus, with a great deal of self-sacrifice, one went about consolidating and maintaining the work. Sir Stanley Rous achieved all this. In recognition of his merits, he was made Honorary President of FIFA in Frankfurt on 11 June 1974.

On that day, the Brazilian Dr. João Havelange took over the reins of the Fédération Internationale de Football Association.

From the moment the South American Confederation, the Confederación Sudamericana de Fútbol, presented his candidature for the FIFA Presidency in 1970, he had looked for solutions to the major problems of world football. When Dr. João Havelange was elected at the 39th Congress in 1974, he was ready to consider football not only as a competition, but also to try and find new ways and means to worldwide technical development and to prepare new generations for this.

Dr. João Havelange's installation in FIFA's headquarters heralded the dawn of a new era. Previously, with survival depending almost exclusively on limited resources from World Championships in four-yearly intervals, FIFA had been somewhat conservative and reserved when it came to taking decisions. Administrative energy had been concentrated on consolidating and maintaining the status quo. In no time, Havelange transformed an administration-oriented institution into a dynamic enterprise brimming with new ideas and the will to see them through. The actual address in Zurich has not altered but instead of the romantic Derwald Villa on the Zurichberg, where in 1974 a staff of twelve used to coordinate the fate of world football, there is now a modern office building housing almost 100 employees coming to grips with an ever increasing workload.

Back in 1974, FIFA was also flexing its muscles in readiness for the tenth World Championship in those days, very much a trial of strength between Europe with nine teams and South America with four. The ripples created by political upheavals, particularly in Africa where many former colonies had been granted independence, were beginning to be noticed on the international sports scene. At that time Africa, Asia, and North/Central America and the Caribbean (CONCACAF) were each still sending one selection to the world's greatest football fiesta. For the 1982 World Cup in Spain, Havelange increased the table of competitors to twenty-four teams. Since that decision, the unqualified success of teams that used to be derided as also-rans has reinforced Havelange's notion that his policies were right. For the 1998 World Cup in France, the number of participating teams was increased to 32 finalists making it the largest in the history of the event, and allowing even greater participation from all its confederations.

On the political level, he firmly followed the course of appeasement and service, following the principle of universality to which FIFA has committed itself. His personal integrity assured Havelange respect from all the national associations and his word carries weight. Under his leadership, the FIFA offices became the hub of sporting diplomacy. An example of this was when representatives from Iraq and Iran, North and South Korea, Japan and Saudi Arabia came face to face in Zurich in July 1993 to discuss the organizational and administrative details for the Asian final qualifiers of the 1994 World Cup in an atmosphere of friendship and peace. Prior to that Havelange had shown a flair for taking advantage of the conciliatory potential of football at exactly the right moment. After intense diplomatic activity, visiting every association at least once and never mincing his words, Havelange soon smoothed the way for the People's Republic of China to return to FIFA. Then, in 1991, both Koreas sent a joint team to the World Youth Championship in Portugal. And because of its particular situation, Israel began competing with European teams in all FIFA qualifying competitions.

Over the past twenty-five years football has not only taken root as the world's major game in an ephemeral world but has also blossomed in other branches of society, commerce and politics. Football, more than any other factor, has enveloped whole regions, people and nations. With approximately two hundred million active players it now constitutes a substantial chunk of the leisure industry, having opened up new markets for itself and for the rest of the business world.

The potential has yet to be exhausted, especially in Asia and North America. As of mid-2000, FIFA has grown to include 204 member associations, thus making it one of the biggest and certainly the most popular sports federation in the world.

On 8 June 1998 Joseph S. Blatter (Switzerland) was elected as the successor to João Havelange (Brazil) as the eighth FIFA President. This victory at the 51st FIFA Ordinary Congress in Paris (France) elevated Joseph S. Blatter, who had already served FIFA in various positions for twenty-three years, onto the highest rang in international football. Joseph S. Blatter is one of the most versatile and experienced exponents of international sport diplomacy and is totally committed to serving football, FIFA and the world's youth.

FIFA World Cup

No other sporting event captures the world's imagination like the FIFA World Cup. Ever since the first tentative competition in Uruguay in 1930, FIFA's flagship has constantly grown in popularity and prestige.

A group of visionary French football administrators, led in the 1920s by the innovative Jules Rimet, are credited with the original idea of bringing the world's strongest national football teams together to compete for the title of World Champions. The original gold trophy bore Jules Rimet's name and was contested three times in the 1930s, before the Second World War put a 12-year stop to the competition.

When it resumed, the FIFA World Cup rapidly advanced to its undisputed status as the greatest single sporting event of the modern world. Held since 1958 alternately in Europe and the Americas, the World Cup broke new ground with the Executive Committee's decision in May 1996 to select Korea and Japan as co-hosts for the 2002 edition.

Since 1930, the 16 tournaments have seen only seven different winners. However, the FIFA World Cup has also been punctuated by dramatic upsets that have helped create footballing history - the United States defeating England in 1950, North Korea's defeat of Italy in 1966, Cameroon's emergence in the 1980s and their opening match defeat of the Argentinean cup-holders in 1990.

Today, the FIFA World Cup holds the entire global public under its spell. An accumulated audience of over 37 billion people watched the France 98 tournament, including approximately 1.3 billion for the final alone, while over 2.7 million people flocked to watch the 64 matches in the French stadia.

After all these years and so many changes, however, the main focus of the FIFA World Cup remains the same - the glistening golden trophy, which is the embodiment of every footballer's ambition.

The last FIFA World Cup was was held from 9 June to 9 July 2006 in Germany, which won the right to host the event in July 2000.Teams representing 198 national football associations from all six populated continents participated in the qualification process which began in September 2003. Thirty-one teams qualified from this process, along with the host nation, Germany, for the finals tournament.

The tournament was won by Italy, their fourth world championship, defeating France 5–3 in a penalty shootout after extra time finished in a 1–1 draw. Germany defeated Portugal 3–1 to finish third.

The 2006 World Cup stands as the most watched event in television history garnering an estimated 26.29 billion non-unique viewers, compiled over the course of the tournament. The final attracted an estimated audience of 715.1 million people.

12

Football in India

Football is one of the most popular games in India. The game commands a massive fan following across the length and breadth of the country. But of late football has lost out to its more illustrious cousin cricket in the popularity stakes. The dwindling interest in the once-popular game is an ample reflection of the shabby state of affairs in Indian football.

At a time when Indian sportspersons are asserting themselves in the world stage and bringing laurels for the country, the Indian football team is languishing at the bottom of the world football rankings. This, despite the fact that India has been Asiad champions in football and have performed commendably well in the Olympics in the 1960s.

The All India Football Federation (AIFF), the governing body in football, introduced the National Football League in 1996 in a bid to raise the standards of the game in India. The effort has met only partial success due to the lack of a comprehensive package to focus on the fitness and tactical dimensions of the players. But a wind of change is blowing in Indian football. The AIFF has roped in Bob Houghton as the new manager of the national team and the Englishman is expected to deliver the goods on account of his associations with some top-ranked Asian teams.

Kolkata, in the state of West Bengal, is considered to be the home of Indian football. The city contains the two most famous Indian teams East Bengal Club and Mohun Bagan AC. Derbies between these two clubs often draw crowds around the 120,000 mark.

Structure of the Game in India

The game in India is administered by the All India Football Federation (AIFF), which is affiliated to the regional Asian Football Confederation, as well as to the worldwide body FIFA. The Indian national team has entered into the regional Asian Cup competition as well as the World Cup. The Indian women's national team has also played in various competitions. Youth football is administered by the governmental Sports Authority of India.

The game is also administered at state levels by state football associations, some of which predate the AIFF. The Indian Football Association, which is responsible for the game in the state of West Bengal, used to be in de-facto charge of the game in India before they pushed for the creation of a national body in association with other state associations. Women's football has its own separate inter-state and state competitions.

The standard of Indian football (compared globally) is poor - the national team is ranked past 100th place in the world, and is said to struggle to qualify for both the World Cup and the Asian Cup. Part of this has been put down to the lack of opportunities for proper training and development of players in the country.

History

During the colonial rule, the Britishers introduced the game of football in India and it rapidly caught the fancy of the native masses. The game found a strong foothold in Bengal with the Mohun Bagan Club coming up in 1889.

The Durand Cup football tournament, the world's third oldest tournament, was started in Shimla in 1898 by the then India's Foreign Secretary, Sir Mortimer Durand. In 1911, the Mohun Bagan Club caused a stir by becoming the first Indian team to lift the IFA Shield, a tournament previously won only by British teams based in India.

Gradually a number of clubs and tournaments proliferated all over the country leading to the formation of the All India Football Federation in 1937. The AIFF got affiliated to the world body FIFA in 1948 and was one of the founder members of the Asian Football Confederation (AFC) in 1954.

The 1951 to 1962 decade was the golden age for Indian football as the country put up a commendable show in a number of international competitions. India won the gold medals in the 1951 and 1962 Asian Games at New Delhi and Jakarta respectively and in the 1956 Melbourne Olympics became first Asian nation to reach the Olympic football semi-final.

The national football team was also quite successful until the 1970s, qualifying for Olympic tournaments and the FIFA World Cup. The team qualified for the 1950 World Cup finals in Brazil, but could not appear as they still played in their bare feet at that time.

The Indian team also won the 1951 and 1962 Asian Games gold medals in football. In 1956 the team finished fourth at the Melbourne Olympics.

All India Football Federation

The All India Football Federation (AIFF) is the apex administrative body governing the game of football in

India. The AIFF is in charge of the national football team and hosts a number of tournaments including the National Football League.

During the initial years of Indian football, in the absence of a central governing body, a bevy of provincial associations called the shots at the regional level. However, the Indian Football Association (IFA), the association governing football in the state of West Bengal, was recognised as the sport's de-facto governing body. By virtue of its affiliation to the Football Association of England, the IFA donned the role of the national body and was at the forefront of various promotional activities.

In 1935, the IFA invited the representatives of the football associations of Assam, Bihar, UP, Delhi, Mysore and Bombay at a conference in Darbhanga, with the aim of forming a national body. But sharp differences among the discussing parties threatened to ruin the conference with the IFA delegates, SN Banerjee and Pankaj Gupta walking out in protest. However, the remaining delegates went ahead and formed the All India Football Association.

In 1937, the warring factions decided to call peace and arrived at a decision to form the All India Football Federation with one representative from each affiliated association and two each from the IFA and the Army Sports Control Board.

National Football Team

The national football team is the national football team of India and is controlled by the All India Football Federation. It is a member of the Asian Football Confederation, and a member of FIFA.

India qualified by default for the 1950 FIFA World Cup as a result of the withdrawal of all of their scheduled opponents. However, they did not take up their place in the competition because FIFA demanded all players at the World Cup finals should wear football boots. A number of the Indian players refused to abide by this rule and the team was forced to withdraw; the team has never since come close to qualifying for the World Cup.

India also finished 4th in the football tournament at the 1956 Melbourne Olympics, and won the 1962 Asian Games Gold medal, and reached the semi-finals in the next two Asian Games tournaments in what became known as the golden era of Indian football.

More recent successes have been limited to the South Asian Football Federation Cup, and the LG Cup won in Vietnam in 2002 under English coach Stephen Constantine.

The Indian team is coached by Englishman Bobby Houghton, who was appointed in June 2006. He has plied his trade for around 30 years in Africa, Asia, the Middle East, North America and Europe with considerable success.

India has several clubs playing association football. Here are some of them. The clubs highlit in bold are national clubs, playing at several national level tournaments apart from India's National Football League (NFL).

Despite football being a highly popular game in India, major victories at the international stage are few and far between. While the national team languishes at the rock bottom of the rankings, the All Indian Football Federation has done precious little to raise the standard of the game in India.

But Indian football has had its share of glory days. India qualified for the 1950 FIFA World Cup in Brazil when all of their opponents withdrew from the competition. However India refused to participate in the event as FIFA required all the players to wear football boots whereas the Indian players were used to playing barefoot.

India made its Olympic debut in football at the 1948 London Games, but lost 1-2 to France in the first match. In the 1956 Melbourne Olympics India became the first Asian nation to reach the semifinals of an Olympic football event defeating Australia 4-2 in the quarterfinal. The hallmark of the win was the hat trick by centre forward Neville D'Souza who became the first and until now only Asian to achieve the feat in the Olympics.

Between 1951 and 1962, during the golden era of Indian football, India was a major power in Asia having won the football golds in the 1951 and 1962 Asian Games at New Delhi and Jakarta respectively and the bronze medal in tile 1970 Bangkok Asiad.

In 2002, India won the LG Cup in Vietnam under English coach Stephen Constantine. India have won the South Asian Football Federation Cup 4 times, in 1993, 1997, 1999 and 2005, but the field features the minnows of Asian football.

Women's Football in India

Women's football has not had the relative head start over the rest of the world that the men's game has had, and also has not had the chance to spread through the country like its male counterpart. The game was administerd by the Women's Football Federation of India (WFFI) until the early 1990s when they were absorbed into the AIFF. However there are complaints that women's football is treated as a poor relation to the men's game leading to (unfulfilled) plans to de-merge the WFFI.

The women's game, like the men's game, also has its early pioneers in the state of West Bengal. The large Kolkata teams, East Bengal and Mohun Bagan, started women's club sides in the 2000/01 season, and they participate with other teams in the Calcutta Women's Football League. However it has been seen recently that players from Manipur have made far advances in the game. Players from these two states make up a large part of the India women's national football team.

The main women's national competition is played on a state vs state basis in the Senior Women National Championship. There are also similar national championships for junior teams: Junior Girls National Championship and the Under-17 Girls National Championship. Some female players have become internationally recognised: in February 2000 Sujata Kar and Alpana Sil became the first Indian footballers to sign a contract outside India itself. They signed with the German team TSV Crailsheim but had to return after a month due to problems with the clearance of their international transfer.

The state of women's football in India, again like its male counterpart, is poor. In the 2003 AFC Women's Championship the Indian team was embarrassed by their results, especially after a 12-0 defeat to the Chinese women's team. This is especially in the light of the poor support by the AIFF, especially of the national team. The team's trip to Germany was only made possible by Non Resident Indians in the country, and by the support of the German Football Association. Furthermore championship are said to be held in remote locations, and national media coverage is said to be lacking with reporting mostly restricted to state and local newspapers.

Famouns Footballers

I. M. Vijayan

Inivalappil Mani Vijayan (born April 25, 1969) is one of the leading Indian football players of modern times.

Vijayan started out as a seller of soda bottles in the Trichur Municipal Stadium, earning 10 paise (0.02 Cents) a bottle. Eventually he was chosen to play for the Kerala Police club and rose to become one of the top names in domestic football. A highly aggressive player, he eventually became the highest earner in Indian club football as well as a regular in the India team. Amongst his achievements in the game Vijayan was crowned Indian Player of the Year in 1992, 1997 and 1999. He also represented the victorious Indian team in the 1999 South Asian Football Federation Cup and scored the fastest international goal in history during the tournament, hitting the net against Bhutan after only 12 seconds. He also finished top scorer in the Afro-Asian Games event held in India in 2003 with four goals. Vijayan's talents attracted interest from clubs in Malaysia and Thailand, although he spent his entire career in India until retirement. Since retiring Vijayan has set a football academy to train young players in his home town.

The unmatching story of Vijayan translated into celluloid in 1999. The film, Kalo Harin, was directed by Cherian Joseph. Other members of the team: A. N. Raveendra Das, N. P. Chandrasekharan (Script), N. P. Chandrasekharan (Lirics), K. Raghavan Master (Music) and P. J. Cherian (Cinimatography). This film finds the life of Vijayan as the struggle for existence and expression by a poor Dalit in mordern India. This film won the National Award and the John Abraham Award in 1999. It also attracted mass appeal in Kerala, the home state of Vijayan at that time. Even though a short non feature film, it was exhibited in local theaters through ticket selling. That was a new episode in the history of Malayalam Film Industry. And, the songs of this film, with their folk touch and Dalit vigour, also became hits then.

After retirement, Vijayan acted as the leading character in internationally acclaimed Indian film "Shantham" (Peace) which won the national award for best film, playing a young man who kills his friend and then is tormented by remorse. He is currently building a reputation for his character roles in Malayalam movies. He is also a member of the National Congress (India).

Baichung Bhutia

Baichung Bhutia (born December 15, 1976 in Tinkitam) is a football player from India. He is known by his fans as the torchbearer of Indian Football in the international arena. He is currently captain of Indian team and plays for Mohun Bagan.

Baichung was born on December 15, 1976 to Dorji Dorma and Sonam Topden in Tinkitam, a sleepy hamlet in South Sikkim district, in the state of Sikkim. As indicated by his surname, he belongs to the Bhutia community.

He started his eduction is St. Xaviers School, Pakyoung, East Sikkim and eventually won a SAI Scholarship to attend the Tashi Namgyal Academy in Gangtok. He went on to play for several school and local clubs in his home state of Sikkim. A stellar performance at the 1992 Subroto Cup brought him to the notice of the football establishment.

In 1993, at the age of sixteen, he left school to join the professional East Bengal Club in Calcutta. In 1995, he moved to JCT Mills, Phagwara, which went on to win the India National Football League that year. Bhutia was a top scorer in the league, and was chosen to play in the Nehru Cup. He was named "1996 Indian Player of the Year", and has won numerous other awards.

In 1997 he returned to East Bengal, and became team captain in the 1998-99 season. In 1999 he travelled overseas to play for Bury F.C. after unsuccessful trials with both Fulham F.C. and Aston Villa F.C. with the move improving his conditioning and strategy. In 2002 he returned to India and played for the Mohun Bagan AC for a year before returning again to the East Bengal Club, and helping them to win the Asean Cup Club Championship. He also signed up to play for Perak, the Malaysian championship club, from August to October of 2003. For the season 06-07 he has again signed for Mohun Bagan AC. He signed an endorsement deal with Adidas India Marketing Pvt. Ltd in November of 2003. Currently he is endorsing Nike India.

Baichung Bhutia married his longtime girlfriend Madhuri Tipnis on December 27, 2004 in his native village of Tinkitam in South Sikkim. The Sikkimese government has built a stadium – the Baichung Stadium in Namchi, the district headquarters, in honour of Baichung. He is one of the most popular figures in the state and is considered as a role model to many Sikkimese and Indians.

Chuni Goswami

Subimal Goswami is a Bengali footballer, and cricketer. He was born in Kishoreganj District, Bengal. As a striker, he played 50 international soccer games representing India. His career begun in 1946, with Mohun Bagan club in Kolkata, where he played until 1968. He also served as the manager of Indian national football team and as the vice president of Mohun Bagan club.

After retiring from soccer, Chuni Goswami focused on playing Cricket. He led Bengal cricket team to the Ranji Trophy final twice. In his cricket career, he played 46 first class matches, scoring 1592 runs and obtained 47 wickets.

Mohammed Salim

Mohammed Abdul Salim (born 1904 in Calcutta, India) was an Indian footballer. Famously the first person from the Indian sub-continent to play for a British football team during a short but significant spell with Celtic F.C.

After being an integral member of Calcutta's Mohammedan Sporting Club side in colonial India, Salim was signed for Celtic by manager Willie Maley after impressing during a trial. Besides being a skilful winger, Salim also became famous for playing the game in bandaged bare feet instead of the customary football boots. On his debut in 1937, Salim helped Celtic win 5-1 against Hamilton Academical F.C. and 7-1 against Galston F.C.

Despite alleged attempts of the club to persuade him to stay, a homesick Salim left Celtic, after only a few months. He returned to Calcutta where he continued his career with the Mohammedan Sporting Club.

Football Tournaments in India

The fact that some of the world's oldest football tournaments are played in India underlines the rich legacy of the game in the country. Over the years, these tournaments, played throughout the year, have been playing host to the skills of India's aspiring footballers.

While Durand Cup, IFA Shield and Federation Cup are major club competitions, Santosh Trophy features various Indian states. But ever since the National Football League has been launched by the AIFF with much fanfare, these prestigious tournaments have been subjected to step-motherly treatment from the football governing body.

Here is a list of domestic football tournaments in India:

— IFA Shield
— Durand Cup
— Federation Cup
— Santosh Trophy

IFA Shield

The Indian Football Association, the association governing football in the state of West Bengal, came into being in 1893 and in the same year the IFA Shield tournament was started.

During the initial years, the IFA Shield, Kolkata's oldest football tournament, was dominated by British army teams. However their stranglehold over the Shield was broken in 1911, when Mohun Bagan became the first Indian team to win the IFA Shield by defeating East Yorkshire Regiment 2-1. That was a historic moment for Indian football as the natives beat the Englishmen at their own game.

East Bengal Club has won the IFA Shield 27 times while their arch rivals Mohun Bagan has bagged the honours 21 times. In the 2005 edition, the second team of German giants Bayern Munich made its debut in the tournament and walked away with the honours by thrashing EverReady SA 5-1 in the final.

Durand Cup

Durand Cup, the oldest football tournament in India, is also 3rd oldest football tournament in the world, after the English FA-Cup and the Scottish FA-Cup.

The Durand Cup football tournament was started in Shimla in 1898 by the then India's Foreign Secretary, Sir Mortimer Durand. Royal Scots Fusiliers bagged the honours in the inaugural Durand cup by defeating Highland Light Infantry with score 2-1.

Since Independence, Mohun Bagan (16) and East Bengal (15) have split 31 cup victories between them. The tournament is hosted by the army and is held at the Ambedkar Stadium in Delhi.

Even though the Durand Cup used to attract huge crowds, the tournament has lost its sheen due to the lack of coordination between the Army and the All India Football Federation (AIFF). With the AIFF investing on the National Football League, like many other domestic competitions, the Durand Cup is also sliding into obscurity.

Federation Cup

Federation Cup is the second most prestigious club football tournament in India after the National Football League (NFL). The tournament was started by the All India Football Federation in 1977 and involves all the major NFL teams.

The 27th edition of the Federation Cup held in Goa in 2005 got a shot in the arm with Zee Sports providing live telecast. In an effort to woo the Indian viewers, Zee employed state-of-the-start broadcasting equipment and a star commentary team.

To bring in the glamour quotient, Zee introduced a group of cheerleaders called the Zeebras.

Santosh Trophy

Before the arrival of the National Football League, Santosh Trophy was India's premier football tournament. The tournament, which was kicked-off in 1941, was named after the late Maharaja Sir Manmatha Nath Roy Chowdhary of Santosh, who had been the President of the Indian Football Association.

In Santosh Trophy, instead of clubs, various Indian states vie for the top honour. In the present format, eight teams that are selected through a qualifying round join the four seeded teams in the quarterfinal league stage. These twelve teams are then divided into four groups of three each and the subsequent group winners complete the semifinal line-up.

The state of Bengal has achieved astounding success in the Santosh Trophy, annexing the title a whopping 29 times.

Bibliography

Daniel W. Drezner, "The Soccer Wars", The Washington Post, Sunday, June 4, 2006, p. B01.

England Premiership (2005/2006), Sportpress. Retrieved on 5 June 2006.

Evans, Alun, *Football on the Edge: The Relationship between Welsh Football Policy-Making and the British International Championship*, M.A. Thesis, De Montfort University, 1996.

FIFA Survey: approximately 250 million footballers worldwide, FIFA official website. Retrieved on 5 June 2006.

FIFA World Cup 2006, FIFA World Cup 2006 website. Retrieved on February 19, 2006.

Football - An Olympic Sport since 1900, IOC website. Retrieved on June 5, 2006.

Frankenberg, Ronald, *Village on the Border: A Social Study of Religion, Politics and Football in a North Wales Community*, London, 1957.

History of FIFA, FIFA website. Retrieved on 3 June 2006.

History of Football, FIFA. Retrieved on 20 November 2006.

Johnes, Martin, 'Irredeemably English?', *Planet: The Welsh Internationalist*, Forthcoming, 1998.

Johnes, Martin, Fred Keenor: A Welsh Soccer Hero, *The Sports Historian*, Forthcoming, 1998.

Johnes, Martin, *That Other Game: A Social History of Soccer in South Wales, c.1906-39*, Univeristy of Wales Ph. D. Thesis, 1998.

Lile, Brian & Farmer, David, 'The Early Development of Association Football in South Wales, 1890-1906', *The Transactions of the Honourable Society of Cymmrodorion*, 1984, 193-215.

Soccer Encarta. Retrieved on May 24, 2007.

The hands-off approach to a man's game. The Times. Retrieved on 3 June 2006.

The History of Offside, Julian Carosi. Retrieved on June 3, 2006.

The History Of The Football League. Football League website. Retrieved on April 19, 2006.

The International FA Board. FIFA website. Retrieved on February 19, 2006.

The World's Most Beloved Sport - The History of Soccer, fussballportal.de. Retrieved on 3 June 2006.

Index